Tidy Your Room

Tidy Your Room

Getting your kids to do the things they hate

Jane Bidder

Editors: Richard Craze, Roni Jay

Viva Books

New Delhi | Mumbai | Chennai | Kolkata | Bangalore | Hyderabad | Kochi | Guwahati

First Indian Edition 2010

VIVA BOOKS PRIVATE LIMITED

- 4737/23 Ansari Road, Daryaganj, New Delhi 110 002
  E-mail: vivadelhi@vivagroupindia.net, Tel. 42242200
- 76, Service Industries, Shirvane, Sector 1, Nerul, Navi Mumbai 400 706
  E-mail: vivamumbai@vivagroupindia.net, Tel. 27721273, 27721274
- Jamals Fazal Chambers, 26 Greams Road, Chennai 600 006
  E-mail: vivachennai@vivagroupindia.net, Tel. 28290304, 28294241
- B-103, Jindal Towers, 21/1A/3 Darga Road, Kolkata 700 017
  E-mail: vivakolkata@vivagroupindia.net, Tel. 22836381, 22816713
- 7, Sovereign Park Apartments, 56-58, K. R. Road, Basavanagudi, Bangalore 560 004
  E-mail: vivabangalore@vivagroupindia.net, Tel. 26607409, 26607410
- 101-102 Mughal Marc Apartments, 3-4-637 to 641, Narayanguda, Hyderabad 500 029
  E-mail: vivahyderabad@vivagroupindia.net, Tel. 27564481, 27564482
- Beevi Towers, First Floor, SRM Road, Kaloor, Kochi 682 018, Kerala
  E-mail: vivakochi@vivagroupindia.net, Tel: 0484-2403055, 2403056
- 232, GNB Road, Beside UCO Bank, Silpukhuri, Guwahati 781 003
  E-mail: vivaguwahati@vivagroupindia.net, Tel: 0361-2666386

www.vivagroupindia.com

Published by arrangement with

Crimson Publishing,
a division of Crimson Business Ltd
Westminster House, Kew Road
Richmond, Surrey TW9 2ND

ISBN : 978-81-309-1496-1

Published by Vinod Vasishtha for Viva Books Private Limited, 4737/23, Ansari Road, Daryaganj, New Delhi - 110 002.

Printed and bound by Raj Press, R-3, Inderpuri, New Delhi - 110 012.

DEDICATION

This book is dedicated to Giles (who doesn't lift a finger); to Lucy (who could run the house); and to William (who has just employed a cleaner for his student pad).

Acknowledgements

Grateful thanks to Oliver Shuster for his painstaking analysis of our *Tidy Your Room* survey.

I would also like to thank my agent Phil Patterson of Marjacq Scripts as well as Roni Jay and Richard Craze for their unfailing good humour and professional attitude.

Finally, I'm extremely grateful to all the parents who were cajoled into filling in our survey when they could have been spending their precious time in nagging their children to tidy their rooms.

Contents

Introduction

"Go and tidy your room!" How often have you said that to your kids without any effect? Face it. You might as well save your breath because even as you're instructing them (all right, yelling at them) to clean the offending bedsit area, they're already doing something much more interesting, like logging on to MSN. And if they do make an attempt to tidy the piles of books, CDs and chewing gum off the floor, they probably won't do it the way you want.

Now all that's about to change. This book holds the secret to getting your kids to do what they don't want to do. Well, maybe that's a bit of an exaggeration but it will definitely help. And as every despairing parent knows, that's a start.

We've divided the first part of this book into age groups because although it would be nice if our five year old learned to change the duvet cover, even the most demanding of us parents needs to recognise that their arms probably aren't long enough. On the other hand, an eight year old might well be more conscientious about washing up than an 18 year old, so if you want to swap ages and chapters, please feel free.

Mind you, however old your kids are, there's one trick that can be applied to all ages. And that's this: *If you learn how to make them WANT to do that job, you've cracked it.*

Now there are all kinds of ways to do this, ranging from bribery to shame, depending on your child's personality and possibly star sign. There's also the winning (or losing) combination of your own personality and theirs. Some parents definitely rub their kids up the wrong way. My 14 year old is constantly telling me I should give him more slack. So part of the trick in getting them to do those jobs they hate, is to change the way you ask them to do it.

Yes, it does sound a bit like politics, doesn't it? But hang on in there, and we'll explain how. Just one more thing before we go on. When your kids refuse to lift a finger, remind them that in the good – sorry, bad – old days, children had to do really tough jobs like plough the land, go up chimneys and sell things in the street. So they've got it easy, now, haven't they?

Chapter one

How to get toddlers to do the things they hate

OK, this might sound a bit like child slavery, but what's wrong with that? Start as you mean to go on and you might just, hormones permitting, have a fairly passable teenager on your hands. Your future daughter-in-law (or son-in-law) will thank you, presuming your untidy little offspring ever finds anyone to take them on.

WHAT YOUR CHILD CAN DO AT THIS AGE

Isn't a toddler too young to enter the work market? Not at all. Under fives can do more than you think. The trouble is that we assume toddlers need us. In fact, they can be a very useful support for adults too. After all, parenting should be give and take, rather like a marriage except that (sadly) you can't divorce the kids.

Here are some examples.

Passing things

'Please can you pass me the remote control?' is a perfectly reasonable request when you've collapsed on the sofa in front of the telly after the school run, cooking dinner, a day in the office and toddler bath time.

Rather like someone learning a foreign language, toddlers can understand more than they can say. So if you point to the remote control and repeat the request, they will eventually get the hang of it. It is, however, vital to remember your own pleases and thank yous. If we don't say it, how can we expect them to reciprocate?

A word of warning, however. Don't criticise them if they drop the control and the batteries fall out, rolling under the sofa to places where you and the vacuum cleaner have never ventured. If you tell them how stupid they are, they won't be very keen to repeat the performance which means that next time, you'll have to get up and get that remote control yourself. Instead, praise them for toddling across the room and tell them how helpful they've been.

There are other things they can pass too. One of the most essential, I have learned over the years, is another roll of loo paper from the cupboard when you are marooned on the seat with one remaining square. Passing the loo roll, however, also requires another skill. You need to make sure they know where such necessities are kept in your house. It's not a bad idea to inform older members of the household at the same time, including any resident husbands or wives and teenagers who presume that new rolls of loo paper arrive like magic.

Collect their own coat/socks/gloves

Yes of course it's quicker to nip up the stairs and get the above items yourself. But if we encourage them at this early age to get their own stuff, they're more likely to carry on when they're older.

Again, this requires a bit of skilful planning on your part. Keep essentials such as coats, socks, gloves, wellies, and slippers close to hand so they don't have to stumble up the stairs and fall down again when retrieving them. This is particularly useful during the panic school run slot when every second counts. I keep a wicker basket of gloves and hats in the hall so they can play lucky dip. They might not end up with matching garments but that's not the point.

Get themselves dressed

Save this one for weekends at first until they improve, as this particular skill can be time consuming – especially if they throw a strop at the same time about what they will and won't wear. One trick is to leave out a choice of gear but always put it in the same place as close to the bed as possible. Start off by making it a game. Isn't it fun? You're going to get out of bed and dress yourself! Yes of course they'll need help with some things but you'll be surprised at how fast they learn.

OK, maybe they won't. So if they need a bit of extra encouragement, try the sing song game. This involves singing out the name of the garment (sock, t-shirt, shorts) as they put it on. It's time consuming which is why we suggest you save this one for weekends but it might just work. And let's face it, even if they only put on some of their clothes, it's a start.

Put their training cup/mug on the table when it's time to eat

Yes, you will need to keep the cup/mug in a place where they can easily reach it. Otherwise you might well be delayed by a trip to casualty. But if they can get into the habit of going to a floor level cupboard and getting their cup, plate and cutlery every time you say 'Please help me lay the table', you're almost there.

It also works in reverse. Don't be so relieved when meal time is over that you allow them to escape, leaving you with all the mess. All right, so they might be a bit young to wash up but they can still pick up their mug and take it to the sink. We agree it's unfortunate if the mug is still full and they spill the contents en route but hey, what's a bit of mess if we're training these kids up for the future?

Put away their toys

This is the first basic step to our ultimate goal of tidying a teenager's tip – sorry, bedroom. The great thing about toddler toys is that they don't usually stick to the floor like gum or other unmentionables to be found in older siblings' dens. So it shouldn't be difficult for a smallish child to pick up a couple of toys and put them somewhere else.

It's the 'somewhere else' that can be the key phrase in the Putting Away Their Toys skill. If you have a bright toy box, kids might be keener to put them in. I have a crafty minded friend who makes her own out of large cardboard boxes. Because her kids have helped her make them, they're keen to use them. She even has one box for puzzles, another for pull along toys and another for little figures. Yes, it *does* sound a bit obsessive but she says it's good for their sorting skills and it keeps them quiet for a while.

Washing up

You have to be a brave parent to do this one as it might involve a certain amount of mess. But that's one of the main points we want to get across. It might be quicker and less messy in the short term if you do it yourself, but if you don't delegate, they won't ever learn. So give them a pinny and maybe a little stool to stand on at the sink and off you go. Alternatively, if you prefer washing, give them a drying up cloth but get them to stick to safe cutlery and avoid glasses.

Clap hands to amuse a younger baby

If you've been brave (careless?) enough to have another baby after your toddler, you might as well make the use of the latter. When mine were little, my eldest son was invaluable in amusing his baby sister with games like Pat a Cake and Funny Faces.

Jobs outside the house

Strapping themselves into the car. Clunk, click. Make it a game. If the little darlings fight the belt, refuse to drive until they put it on. Alternatively, get older children to do this job for the younger ones. (Always make sure it's done up properly before you drive off.)

Holding shopping. Nothing heavy, you understand, or someone will be onto ChildLine. But they could carry the odd tin for you.

Paying up

Most children love playing shop. So let older pre-schoolers help you find the right change if your shopping isn't big enough to warrant a credit card. It also teaches them the difference between coins.

WARNING *Do not, on any account, let them find out what your pin number is. A certain child of my acquaintance (not my own – honestly) topped up his mobile phone credit courtesy of his father's plastic. And he wasn't even nine years old.*

Look for a car parking space

My lot used to love this 'job' when they were small. First one to call out 'There's one' got loads of praise.

On the job thinking

When you're doing jobs yourself, ask yourself if your children are old enough or capable enough to help you with whatever you're doing at the time. It might give you some ideas.

HOW TO GET THEM TO DO IT

This is where we enter the heavy psychology bit. Actually, it's not that heavy – we're just trying to sound knowledgeable. In fact, it's common sense with a very large dash of parental cunning.

Explain why it needs to be done

I have a friend who has always logically explained to her children why they should wash their hands after the loo, clean their teeth, and not run across the road. She's very calm and will quietly point out what will happen if they do and don't do these things.

She also does the same with jobs that they're not keen on. For example, if they don't want to put away their toys, she will tell them that someone might trip over them and hurt themselves. Or that they won't be able to find them the next day. Personally this never worked on my children because they're too strong minded but it's worth starting off with the logical approach before you try other tactics.

Praise them/thank them so they want to do it again

If you're sitting marooned on the loo seat and your toddler actually manages to get off their backside to pass you another roll of paper, believe me you'll be grateful. Toddlers are vain people. If someone praises them, they'll want to do it again. So make sure they know how grateful you are. And tell them what clever little sausages they are, as well.

Also sing their praises in front of other people – when the kids can hear you. It will make them feel good and make them want to repeat the performance.

Give them their own equipment

Embroider/write their name on a drying up cloth which can then be their very own. In fact, we think this is such a good idea that we might just start manufacturing our own White Ladder for Kids drying up cloths.

Make it into a game

Who can tidy their bedroom faster? Who can clear up their pile of toys before someone else? You could even offer small rewards. Another idea is to hide little treats round the room which they can find as they clean or tidy up. A kind of treasure hunt with ulterior motives.

Water play

Water games usually go down well so use this in conjunction with jobs. Put a bowl of soapy water in the garden, if it's a nice day, or on a sheet of paper on the kitchen floor. Get them to scrub down bath toys or anything else that's washable.

Stage your own musical

Put on the radio or get them to sing while they're doing jobs. I know a mum – honestly – who will stand in the middle of her children's room and point out areas that need tidying while at the same time, singing Do, Ray, Me etc. from the Sound of Music. And it works even though she does look a bit like a musical conductor.

Bribery

This one's a bit tricky as you don't want to start too young or you could be paying out thousands by the time they're teenagers. You also need to follow through your bribe so if you promise them an ice cream if they get themselves dressed all on their own, you mustn't fulfil your side of the bargain if they haven't fulfilled theirs. And don't even contemplate 'forgetting' to keep your promise when they have done all they can to keep their side of the bargain.

Bribes don't have to be based on money. They could be treats like a trip to the park or the ice cream van.

Stick to a routine

Children feel comforted by routine – as do many adults. So incorporate certain jobs into your daily family routine. Explain to your children from as early an age as possible that after they have finished eating and it's gone down, they help you clear the table. After they've got dressed, they fold their pyjamas and pull up the duvet. After their bath, they clean their teeth and hang up their towel to dry.

WHAT TO DO WHEN THEY WON'T CO-OPERATE

We think this section is very important. We personally hate parenting books that presume readers have children who will do what they are told. This only happens in fairy tales or very boring families. My three all have minds of their own, which is why White Ladder asked me to write this book. So here's what to do if, or when, they won't play ball.

Empathise, empathise, empathise

"Tell them you understand how they feel," says psychologist Gaynor Sbuttoni who is also a mother of three. "Say 'Yes, I know it's boring to tidy your room and I can understand that you don't know where to start because it is a bit of a mess, isn't it? But if you do this pile first and then this one…' That way, you're keying into their wavelength by showing them you're on their side. You're also providing a practical way out of their dilemma by suggesting a strategy."

Provide an incentive

They might be too young for bonuses (that comes in another section) but you can encourage them with a little handout on the quiet. Keep a bag of stickers or sweets or whatever that they can dip their sticky little hands into when they've performed that job. No, only one!

Show them the consequences

Oh dear, has someone trodden on your favourite toy and broken it? That's because you didn't put it away safely. We're not suggesting you break a toy on purpose but if it happens, it happens. And of course, if you happen to stumble over a toy and break your ankle, someone else is going to have to look after the kids, aren't they? Actually, that's one way to get a break (all puns intended).

Appeal to their desire to be grown-up

Say 'That's a shame, I thought you'd be big enough to do that.' Most toddlers want to be grown-up unless they're reverting to babyhood, thanks to a new brother or sister. If that's the case, tell them you'll ask the baby to do it. That should get them going. (It will make all the child psychologists write into us too.)

IT WORKED FOR US! PARENTS' TIPS

A problem shared is a problem halved. If we all confided in other parents about difficulties, we might get some more ideas on how to tackle them. So we've spent several months interviewing parents all over the country on how they get their kids to tidy up. Here are some of their suggestions.

"My son is now eight but since he was two and a half, he has loved helping with 'a job'. I had to try and do the washing up quietly so he didn't join in because there would be too much water to clear up afterwards. And he likes nothing better than to empty my cupboards so he can tidy them. I think he liked it because it was something we could do together and actually, it was preferable for me to do this than sit on the floor playing cars. To get kids to help with housework, I'd suggest turning it into a competition such as who can make their room the tidiest and who would like a turn with my broom?"

Jane

"I have a two year old daughter who has started taking an interest in helping me clean. It is really hard to get it done but one thing I have done is give her a duster and then I have one and she helps me polish. It's all about involvement and making things fun. She is also starting to take an interest in what we are cooking and likes to watch things cook. For Christmas, I plan to buy her a toy vacuum cleaner which I hope she will want to use whilst I use mine."

Helen

"I got my children, aged seven and three, to start helping when they were three but it wasn't slave labour. I presented it as 'helping me' or making it into a game. If they don't want to help, I operate a quid pro quo scheme. So I'll say that if they don't tidy up after themselves, I won't take them to the park or let them play Playstation etc."

Louisa

"We have a system of counting to encourage our three year old to focus on something. For example, she tidies the room while I count to ten. I'll count to five while she gets her shoes on. It works very well. If we're out and she doesn't want to go home, she knows that if

I start to count, I'm serious and she always comes. It also works for stopping unwanted behaviour. Stop before I count to three." (*Author's note: Wonder how long this will last…*)

Anne

Top tip

When the novelty wears off, count in a different language.

"I was widowed two years ago and afterwards, I didn't care about rules and discipline because I was too depressed. Now I'm trying to claw back some structure in the house and it's very hard. It's also difficult as a single parent because you have no one to back you up. And if you're extremely tired, there comes a point where you just give in and say 'All right then, don't bother.'"

Caroline

"I get my children, aged 10, seven and three to put their pyjamas under their pillows. It's only a small job but it's something the little one can do."

Sarah

Sarah Beeny, television presenter, says: "I ask my 18 month old son Billy to put things in the rubbish bin, in an excited voice. He's usually willing to do this. The only trouble is that he puts lots of other things – which I haven't asked him to – into the bin as well and then expects a similar amount of praise!"

Key points

- *Start young* The sooner you do, the less they are likely to question. And they'll be used to helping as they grow up. Make the most of this impressionable age
- *Make it fun* Try to make jobs a nice thing to do and not a boring chore. You can do this with music and imaginative games

- *Remember you're helping their brain develop* This isn't just a book on child slave labour. Doing jobs can help their minds grow
- *Be imaginative* There are all kinds of jobs that even small children can do

Chapter two

How to get four to eight year olds to do the things they hate

The good news about this age group is that they can usually understand what you're asking them to do. The bad news is that they've learned to say 'no'. Our mission is to find an in between route so that you win but they think it's a compromise.

WHAT YOUR CHILD CAN DO AT THIS AGE

*Fit the batteries into the remote control and other electrical apparatus**

The great thing about having small children is that they have small hands which can get into places that bigger hands can't – like that fiddly bit at the back of the remote control. Kids are also often more technically wired up than we are so as well as fitting the batteries, they can also tell us how to work the remote control if we're still at the manual stage. I know one parent who actually woke up one of his sleeping children to help him out with a DVD that he couldn't operate. That's going a bit far but, as he said, it made his son feel good about himself because he could do something his dad couldn't.

Lay the table

The trick about this one is that they learn to do it as a habit. Don't just save it to impress your mother/sister/visitors and then feel embarrassed when the kids say they don't know where the cutlery is

***WARNING** *Please make sure it is safe for them to do this.*

kept. Teach them where to find things and make it routine for them to get the table ready before you eat.

Clear their own plate after a meal

Again, schedule this into the general dos and don'ts of eating like not eating with your mouth open. Make sure they know where the bin is and try to get them to aim straight so you don't have to do the floor again. Ideally, then get them to head for the dishwasher if you have one. And yes, to put the plate in and not on it…

Hang up their clothes

Start now and you might just instill the habit. One of my friends colour codes her kids' clothes on a hanging rail. Her children actually enjoy finding the right section to hang their clothes in.

Top tips

- Get or make novelty hangers so the kids want to use them
- Make sure that wardrobes and drawers are within their reach. If they're inaccessible, it's too easy for them to say 'I can't do that'. Those slide-under-the-bed drawers are great for kids because they're easy to pull in and out. Buy the kind that don't require runners. You can get them from John Lewis and other stores
- Put up low level clothes hooks so they can hang up their own coats. Write their name on a wooden clothes peg so they can 'peg' together their Wellington boots

---

Put their clothes in the dirty linen bin

Sounds obvious but make sure they know where it is. Make it part of their bath routine. When they get out, they put their discarded dirties in the right place. Don't just bend down and do it yourself because it's quicker or they'll never learn. Teach younger children to tuck one sock into the other so they don't go missing.

Load the dishwasher – and unload it too

All right. This might be a bit tricky for a four year old but you can start off with plastic cups and cutlery that won't hurt them. This does, however, require a bit of teaching first. Everyone has their own idea of how to put in plates and knives so train your kids up in your way of thinking.

Top tip

Don't let them get away with it if they claim they didn't load the dishwasher because they didn't know if it was clean or dirty. Get them to open up and see which one it is. It's not difficult.

Tidy their room

You're going to find this in all the age group sections because it's an essential skill – right through to adulthood. Four to eight year olds are still, hopefully, a bit more biddable than teens so make the most of it. Buy brightly coloured plastic crates for them to store toys/CDs/other stuff in. Every few weeks, encourage them to have a purge and throw out/give away things they don't want.

Top tips

- Get them to make labels like CDs/Musical toys/games to stick on the boxes
- Be specific. Don't just say 'tidy your room'. Point out certain things which need to be put away such as clothes or toys. Alternatively, divide the room into sections and get them to tidy one at a time. Don't make them do it all at once or it will seem too daunting. See chapter Five for how to teach your child tidying skills.

Take down the Christmas decorations and store them in boxes

Get them to write labels on the side.

Moving house?

Help them get used to the idea by giving them a box and getting them to pack some of their own things. Again, label and even decorate the label.

Use a wipe on/wipe off board

Or you could use a magnetic calendar to remind them what jobs they have agreed to. Reminding them to do something doesn't mean they're forgetful or naughty. It's natural. As parents, we need to keep reminding them again and again.

Jobs outside the house

Cleaning their bikes

Give them a sponge and an old washing up bowl. Show them how to get round the spokes.

Sweeping up leaves

Give them the right tools and show them where to put them. Use the opportunity to show them the different kind of trees.

Picking up apples from the ground

Sort out the baddies. Get them to help you cook an apple pie with the good ones, as an incentive. Get them to put the bad ones on the compost.

Picking flowers for the house

Get them to pick flowers for the table or guest room when you have visitors.

Cleaning out your car

Provide them with two old carrier bags. One for rubbish and another for things that belong inside the house. Check both afterwards to make sure they haven't thrown important things away.

Top tip ______________________________

Encourage them to do this by allowing them to keep any small change they find.

HOW TO GET THEM TO DO IT

We've already given you some ideas in the previous section for toddlers. These can be expanded for this age group.

Explain why it needs to be done

If you don't unload the dishwasher, we won't have any clean cups next time you want a drink.

Praise and thank them when they do it

If you don't, why should they do it again?

Give them their own equipment

Instead of the family dirty linen bin, give them a string bag and get them to put their own dirties in it.

Bribery

By the age of five, it's a good idea to start giving them pocket money so they learn the value of money. It's also a great incentive for jobs round the house. Link the jobs with the pocket money. If they don't do certain jobs, they don't get the money. If they do, they get a bit extra. We'll leave the details up to you, depending on your parenting style and budget (and see chapter 15).

Pocket money isn't the only way to bribe them. Is there something they really want? If so, use that to their (and your) advantage. For example, if they want to redecorate their bedroom, they can choose a new duvet if they promise to keep their bedroom tidy for the rest of the school term. But they have to stick to their side of the bargain.

Non-financial incentives

Draw up a list of privileges that they can earn if they do certain jobs. For example, if they lay the table, they don't have to help load the dishwasher.

Make it into a game

Who can lay one side of the table faster than the other?

Crack a few jokes

I don't know about you but I generally fail to see the funny side when my kids don't listen. So recently, I've introduced a new rule: make a joke every day. However, as my kids say my jokes are pathetic, this doesn't always work. Instead, I've resorted to a wry sense of humour which often comes out of my mouth before I've analysed it. The other day, my 14 year old tore into the house wearing very muddy trainers. "Take your feet off," I yelled without thinking. He thought that was quite funny and now I use that instruction instead of the much more boring 'Take off your shoes'.

Ask them in another language

This is not, by any means, guaranteed to get the job done but it might be enough for them to turn round and say 'Wot are you on?' Hopefully, younger children will be more impressed and it might even help their French or German. I often insert the odd French word so they get the rough idea. Try these phrases for size. 'Will you get out of le lit?' Or 'Tidy your chambre, s'il vous plait.'

Star charts

Put it on the wall and fill it in daily. Make a list of the jobs you want them to do and whether or not they've done them. Give them rewards at the end of the week. Use a wipe on/wipe off board or magnetic board to list chores they have agreed to do. It's natural for children to need to be reminded about a job.

WHAT TO DO WHEN THEY WON'T CO-OPERATE

Get the punishment to fit the crime

If they won't lay the table, they won't have a place to sit at. Sounds a bit tough? Maybe. But how difficult is it to put out a mat?

Teach them the consequences

If they won't tidy their bedroom, they won't be able to find that toy they've been looking for.

Ask why they won't do it

If they hate that job so much, maybe they could trade it for another. If it's a 'Can't be bothered' attitude, explain we all have to do things we don't like at times. Get them to think what would happen if you went on strike and never cooked/washed/ironed/unloaded the dishwasher. Even better, try this for a day and see what happens.

Show them up

If your child won't help, persuade a visiting child to hand you that nappy/pass the trainer mug. Then praise them and give them a small reward. There's nothing like the green eyed monster to gain co-operation and next time, your child might come up trumps. Naughty but it works.

Put them down for a legal career

They can make money by arguing against logic.

IT WORKED FOR US! PARENTS' TIPS

"I tell my six and seven year olds that the more they do to help me, the more time we will have to do fun things together. I also show them that some chores can be quick."

Mandy

"Our eight and six year olds tidy their rooms and make their own beds. If they won't, we say we'll take something away or they'll lose a treat."

Sally

"I have a 'Wonka Bar' chart named after Roald Dahl's Charlie and the Chocolate Factory. It works a dream round the house. There are four columns on the chart: one for me, one for my husband and one each for the children. Then there's a list of all the things I do round the house that they could help with. Ten ticks on the chart earn you a chocolate bar if you're an adult. For children, it works according to age. For example, my son is six so he just needs six ticks. Alternatively, if they don't want a chocolate bar they can have £1 pocket money. My family soon sussed out the easy ticks and so making beds and laying the table are done like a dream. My husband takes the recycling down the garden and has made the bed for the first time in 13 years of marriage! My daughter now has a tick for practising the piano which I always hate nagging about. I, of course, end up with hundreds of ticks but psychologically, this has worked well for me as everyone can see all the jobs I do every day."

Giselle

"My four year old dusts as a game. She also 'plays' at gardening and enjoys helping her dad make dinner sometimes."

Hollie

"I get our six and four year olds to tidy their rooms and load the dishwasher by bribing them with television or letting them stay up later. Mine are still small enough that if I stand there looking menacing for long enough, they eventually give in and do it. I think mothers who work (and I'm one) feel guilty about being away from their children and when they're with them, they don't want to upset their kids or cause tension or fights so the kids get away with far more. You have to remember who's the boss. I also try and remember my mother getting me to do things. Stand firm and think of a suitable sanction if they don't do it. One of my friends brings all the clean washing into her girls' room and they put it all away. That's their job and if they do it, they get their pocket money. If not, they don't."

Anon

"Our children are aged seven and five. They tidy their rooms, help with younger children, water houseplants and garden. If they won't help, we threaten them with 'No TV'. Threats and praise also help."

Anon

"I insist my children do jobs and explain they need to know how to look after themselves when they leave home. I expect boys to do the same as girls as I think so many relationships are ruined by men who expect everything done for them. I also use a system of rewards. For example, I think of something they want and only give it if they do what I've asked. I also make them use the washing machine for their own clothes. I suppose I see them as equal to me but needing training to do things and explaining why. I also try to help them see the positive side of their failures – such as showing them that something shrank because they put it on the wrong setting but that they can do it better the next time."

Lynne

"When my children were this age, I used to encourage them to match odd socks in the laundry basket by buying them a pile of Pokemon cards and handing over one card for every pair of socks they matched up. Being boys, they were quite competitive and I could sit and drink coffee while they turned the house upside down. As a keen but lazy gardener, I also offered a 5p bounty for every slug they found and disposed of, for me. This one worked best when they could hear the ice cream van a few streets away. When they got older, of course, this didn't work. Then I would give them a choice. Do you want to wash the car or the dog? Do you want to do the dishes or hang out the washing? This last one worked particularly well. As I have three boys, they could not allow their friends to see them hanging out the washing so they would always choose the other option, whatever that was. My children, unlike my friends' kids, never said they were bored. That's because the first time they said it at the start of the school holidays, I found them something to do like weeding, cleaning, putting the laundry away. If they protested, I pointed out that they had just complained they had nothing to do."

Jacqui

"I expect my sons to do as much as my daughters as I think too many men expect their wives to run after them."

Anon

"My daughter has a tick list for piano practice. When she gets to seven ticks, she gets a small present."

Helen

"My four year old granddaughter refused to carry her baby sister's soiled nappy downstairs from the bathroom to the outside bin, even though it was sealed in a plastic bag. I got round this by saying 'Oh please help granny. I can't manage the baby unless you do.' It worked because she could see I needed a hand."

Susan

"Our eight year old is borderline special needs and genuinely finds being organised or tidy an enormous problem. So we don't set an objective level of tidiness for all the kids to achieve but set him a 'target' that stretches *him* while still being attainable. So if he tidies the floor, we'll tidy the rest of the room. This has led us to think more generally in terms of individual standards that are challenging but not unreasonable for all tasks. For example, our six year old is helpful but lazy so he's expected to achieve quite a lot but is allowed to tackle tasks in short bursts."

Maddie

"Our eight and six year old regularly lay and clear the table for meals, get drinks for the family before meals and tidy their bedrooms. I expect them to do it because it's the way the household works. You also have to be specific. 'Tidy your room' is too vague. You need to give instructions like putting your clothes in the cupboard; putting books on the bookshelf; putting toys in a box. Decide on boundaries and compromise. Plates have to be put in the dishwasher by everyone, but if it's not your room and not your mess, it's not your problem if it's not tidied to your standards. Only have a few rules for the things that are really important to you."

Sue

"We introduce a bit of competition between siblings – mean but effective – such as who can tidy their room the best? Of course, they are both winners in the end but the thought of winning keeps them going. I also make jobs into a challenge, for example 'I bet you can't finish tidying by the time the timer goes off' or 'When you've finished, there'll be a surprise treat for everyone'. It might just be one sweet but the suspense keeps them going. We never *ever* pay for jobs round the house. This is a slippery slope. We generally work on incentives like 'When you've done that, we can go to the park'."

Jenny

" My eight year old picks up her clothes but as I work full time and don't get home until 6.30, I don't feel it's appropriate to expect too much. I would far rather she has some playtime and then time for a story. I also think it's important to look at what needs to done across the week, rather than expecting to get everything done on the day. Children like to know what's planned. I believe in reward charts and goals. Also saving up stickers for a treat."

Laura

(For more about reward charts see page 26.)

"I never give up with my children aged six and two, because then they'd never do anything. I tend to join in so we do it together. I find it helps if the children choose their own jobs. For example, my daughter likes dusting the television and sees it as 'her' job so she's quite keen to do it. This also gives a child more of a sense of control and independence. As a last resort, I will sometimes say that if things are left on the floor, then I'll assume she doesn't want them and throw them away. Then they get picked up fairly fast. I've never actually followed through on this one although their dad has. At school, they play fast music during 'tidy up' time. I'm also a NeuroLinguistic Programming Practioner, so I'm very aware of the language I use and its effects. In practice, I am more likely to tell them what I want them to do, rather than telling them off for doing the wrong things. I generally focus on praising good behaviour. At the end of the day, children want your undivided attention and they will do whatever it takes to get this. They don't judge by what is naughty and what isn't. We do that instead."

Joanne

"Over Christmas we got fed up with family who descend, enjoy our hospitality and then leave without even putting so much as a plate in the sink. Especially those with no kids and no responsibilities – in other words the ones for whom Christmas is relaxing rather than exhausting. We decided we didn't want our kids to grow up behaving like that towards other people. So the new rule is that whenever we have a proper family meal together (in our case probably three or four times a week) no one leaves the kitchen after the meal until all the clearing up is done. It doesn't matter what job everyone does, but it isn't fair for one person to put their feet up while someone else is still working. So the children, being little, can do fun or easy jobs like loading the dishwasher (which they seem to enjoy for some reason), putting away the condiments or wiping the table, while we break our wrists scrubbing at the burnt pots and pans (as they get older this may change), but the principle is that we all start together and we all finish together. They have yet to find any way of arguing against the fairness of this, and so far it's working well."

Richard

Radio 1 DJ *Judge Jules*, aka Julius O'Riordan, has a six year old son, Jake. He says:

"Jake cleans his bedroom but that's about the long and the short of it. We persuade him to do it by threatening to cancel whatever fun activity is planned for that forthcoming weekend. When I was a child, I did loads of jobs. I swept up leaves, washed up, tidied up, ironed and put washing on the line."

REWARD CHARTS

Some parents believe in these and others don't. Although they can encourage some children, they can also demoralise others if they don't get the results. And it can damage their self-esteem if someone else gets more points than them every time.

Dr Jill Curtis, child expert and psychotherapist, says "Star charts can be most effective *for some children.* If this reward doesn't seem to work for your child – and for many it does not – don't worry, but try to work out another way of marking success. It could be as simple as praise from you. Words do count."
www.familyonwards.com

Key points

- *Keep going* and don't give up. If you let them off something, they'll refuse to do it next time
- *Build on the jobs* they've already been doing
- *Praise, praise them* Every child and adult is encouraged by this
- *Remind, remind, remind* Don't expect your children to remember every time that they're meant to be doing something. But don't nag them so they're turned off

Chapter three

How to get eight to 12 year olds to do the things they hate

Uh, oh. We're getting into the almost-teens territory here. Which is why it's even more important to get them into the habit of doing some work for their living. The trick is emotional intelligence. Get them to want to do those jobs – even if it's for money.

JOBS THEY CAN DO

Vacuum the carpet (not the cat)

They could start off with vacuuming their own bedrooms and then move onto others. However, a few driving lessons might be necessary first or you could find them slicing off part of the woodwork in their enthusiasm or reluctance to do it properly.

Some clever toy companies actually make mini vacuum cleaners. You can even purchase toy vacuum cleaners. However, it's cheaper to buy them a dustpan and brush. In fact, their nimble little fingers are probably far better at getting into spaces you can't reach.

Dust their bedroom

This might sound a bit tough but if they don't start now, they might not ever. Present them with a duster and, if they're the kind of child who might abuse solvents, put some polish on it for them. Suggest they move objects round on their dressing tables or desks in the process.

Clean their own shoes

Well, you didn't get them dirty, did you? Make it easy for them with those packets of shoe shine polishes. Allocate one day of the week, like Sunday, for them to do it.

Match socks

Isn't it amazing how socks come apart in the wash? But now you've got your little helper to put it right. So the next time they say they're bored, suggest a sock matching game. And when they've finished their own underwear drawer, they can do everyone else's too.

Clean the car

Not just the inside but the outside too. Get them togged up in clothes that you don't mind getting dirty and wet. Provide them with a bowl of water or a hosepipe and leave them to it.

Make their own packed lunches

Help them, if necessary by putting out the right ingredients.

Put the kettle on

This is a bit of a grey area as you also need to warn them about boiling water. But they've got to start somewhere. And once they've got the hang of it, you can then teach them to make tea although we'd recommend you save this for the 10 year age group upwards. They'll probably like this job as it will make them feel grown-up.

Other basic culinary skills

Make toast. But do teach them basic safety rules first such as only toasting ready sliced bread in case they try to stick in bread that's too thick. Never, ever try to get the toast out with a knife or they could get electrocuted. They could also learn to make their own school sandwiches although you might regret this in the early morning rush when they're deliberating between peanut butter and jam, or both.

Change the ringer on your mobile phone

Explain how to retrieve missed calls etc. In fact, they'll love this job and we have to throw in the odd perk so they want to do some of the jobs they hate.

Top tip

Look out for some great cookery cassettes called Cooking For Kids. They were actually thought up by a former war correspondent who changed careers. In our book, kids can be as challenging as war zones so maybe he's on the right track.

Teach them how to fold napkins into fancy shapes

Not a vital job, we admit, but they might enjoy it and it would raise your street cred at dinner parties.

Change their bedlinen

This might be a bit of a tough one at this age but you can start by getting them to replace their pillow cases. In the next age range, they can move on to duvets.

Amuse younger children

When my eldest was this age, he was brilliant at this. In fact, I don't think I could have managed without him. The great thing about older children being entertainers/substitute nannies, is that they don't have to do much. They simply have to make silly faces or be cool or play the odd game. Younger kids normally think they're so wonderful that they take it all in.

WARNING *Never leave a child of this age unattended with younger children for obvious reasons. If you're in the house but not in the same room, keep a regular check on them.*

Help carry the shopping

Don't assume it's all too heavy. Give them a couple of things in a carrier bag. Encourage them to help you pack at the supermarket by giving them their own plastic bags to fill, and let them pack their favourite foods.

Take visitors' coats

Preferably not to sell on eBay but to save them until going home time.

Unload the dishwasher

But teach them to avoid sharp knives etc. A trip to Casualty will only make you late for the next job.

Sort out the rubbish

And understand how the recycling bin works.

And don't forget jobs from previous sections which are still applicable to this age group.

HOW TO SELL IT TO THEM SO THEY AGREE TO DO IT

Start off with the basics.

Why they need to do it

If they don't change their pillow cases, their bed gets smelly.

Praise them for the things they do

It will make them keener to do other jobs.

Give them their own equipment

How about a pair of rubber gloves with their name on a clothes peg to keep them together? Or a pinny with their name on it?

Bribe

But don't give away money for small favours. The little-by-little approach makes them try hard more consistently. You can do this in different ways. Put a price tag on each job, for example making the bed every day gets 10 pence. Give them a set amount of pocket money every week but only if they do the list of jobs you've both agreed.

Allow them to change their room around

Or give it a makeover. It might encourage them to keep it tidy, or at least sort out the rubbish before they change it.

Permit them to tidy out your briefcase

And/or handbag in return for tidying up their own school bag. Agree they can keep loose change that they find, as payment.

Give them a choice of jobs

This usually works best when it's written down rather than agreed verbally. That way, they can see what they've agreed to do. A list is the obvious way to do this. But you could also try a 'lucky dip' jam jar filled with pieces of paper, each of which has a job on. Every day, every member of the family has to pull out a 'job ticket'. They might loathe the job – or they might like it. That's part of the fun.

Banking bonuses

Sit down as a family and work out which jobs can be done by which members of the family. Write down a core list of important jobs under each individual's name. These jobs 'have' to be done or else their salary (in other words, pocket money) doesn't get paid. If extra jobs are done willingly on top of this, you agree to pay a bonus.

Crack better jokes

Or you could say things in a funny voice. Try holding your nose and coming out with a squeaky command. They'll think you're mad but it might grab their attention for a few seconds. Use that time fast to connect their ears to their brains.

WHAT TO DO IF THEY WON'T CO-OPERATE

Don't give in and do it yourself

The next time they ask you to do something, explain you can't agree because they didn't do the job you asked them to do. Stick to it.

Explain the consequences

If they won't help amuse the younger children, it means you'll take longer getting out and then they'll be late for something they want to get to.

Work shamelessly on their consciences

They helped to make the car dirty by chucking all that rubbish in the back so they ought to help clean it out.

IT WORKED FOR US! PARENTS' TIPS

"It was a horrible rainy day so I got the kids to tidy out the kitchen drawers. I've got one which is full of miscellaneous things that don't seem to belong anywhere, like rubber bands and loose change. They actually enjoyed sorting it out and I let them keep the change as a reward."

Michelle

"Mine are still quite small – eight and five – but they do have a responsibility to keep their rooms tidy. It's usually prompted by me saying 'Look, I can't see the floor and I need to vacuum the carpet. You have a choice. Tidy your stuff away or it goes in a big black bag and in the dustbin. They also know they're expected to help clear the table after meals and put their own dirty laundry in the laundry basket. However, this sometimes needs a reminder. Other than that, because I'm a writer, I believe deadlines come before dusting. So they probably don't have a good example of doing jobs round the house!"

Kate

"We drew up a loyalty chart, based on the supermarket loyalty card schemes. Every time the children do a job, we give them so many points. After a certain number of points, they get a free gift. But I do think that girls are better at doing jobs round the house than boys."

Laura

"Our children are aged eight, 10 and 12 and they do lots of jobs round the house. But they differ. One enjoys tidying her room; one hates it. They all hate scraping leftovers off the plate to load the dishwasher. We link jobs with pocket money but sometimes they turn down some jobs and go without the money. We also warn children when they'll be expected to do a task. Don't expect them to drop what they're doing. Star charts and reward systems work, but need commitments. Lots of praise and helping with the task is important as young children need to know how to do things more than we realise. So show them how to tidy a room without just shoving everything into the wardrobe. Make tasks into a family occasion; the children have enjoyed clearing up the garden together or cleaning the house when we are expecting visitors, if we all work together. Don't expect to achieve these ideals all the time. All families nag and grumble sometimes."

Carole

"Ours are nine and five. We get them to do jobs by linking it to a reward or punishment. For example, we either promise some form of treat or threaten a prohibition of a favoured pastime/thing until the job is complete. We also tend to put time limits and deadlines on the activities."

Brian

"My nine and 12 year olds tidy their rooms, sometimes load the dishwasher, make their own beds, dust, vacuum and do the ironing even though it often needs doing again. Praise helps and so do threats. If they really refuse, I don't give them pocket money."

Anon

"The only way to get my 13,11 and eight year olds to do jobs is to stand over them and threaten them with a smack! Seriously, try making it fun and light-hearted. Also try timing them for a bit of healthy competition and barter with them too. If they'll do this for you, you'll do that for them."

Anon

"Our nine year old tidies his bedroom, empties wastepaper bins and lays the table. He has to do seven chores each week to earn his pocket money. Some parents might say that offering money for household chores will lead to an expectation for all housework to be paid. But by defining which chores are eligible to count towards the pocket money requirement, we've been able to avoid this problem."

Susie

"It's all about communicating with your children as burgeoning people – not as inferior beings who have to be kept in line. They need to grasp the connection between having a nice lifestyle and doing certain things in order to achieve it. That's best taught by example. I also only give them pocket money and time out when jobs are completed satisfactorily."

Caroline

"Sometimes, we just have to stand there until our seven and ten year olds do the jobs we've asked them to."

Anon

"Try to instill a sense of the benefits of a clean and tidy house e.g. if you don't trip over things, you can find things. By making these things a family activity, a sense of responsibility will hopefully grow.

A friend also gave us a great idea. Each member of the family has a box which is kept in the same place, like under the stairs. As you go about your daily business and you find something that is somewhere it shouldn't be, you just put it into the relevant box. At the end of the week, empty the box into a pile on the bed so the person is forced to clear it away. Works like a dream on my wife!"

Brian

"We've only just started getting our seven and 10 year olds to do jobs in the last few months so we've been building up slowly. I pick my battles and only get them to do jobs I really want them to do. I say 'I'm your guide, not your slave'. I also tell them that if they don't tidy up their toys, they will go into a big black bag. I also highlight choice and consequence. If their toys get broken when someone stands on them, it's because they should have put them away. At the same time, I tell myself that the world won't end if their rooms aren't tidy every night. I also think you have to tailor tactics to each child. My two are like chalk and cheese; what motivates one, will often antagonise the other. I'm a great believer in sticking to your guns: once you've said they have to do something, don't let them off until they do it. Lead by example, be fair and consistent especially when they're not. And keep your sense of humour nearby."

Cass

Anthea Turner, stepmother of three girls aged nine, 12 and 13 and presenter of *The Perfect Housewife* on BBC3, says: "Leadership is the main key. As the saying goes: 'A fish rots from the head down.' In other words, if they don't see you doing it, they won't do it either. So the standards have to be set by the head of the household. If you leave wet towels on the bathroom floor, so will they. If your bedroom is a mess, why should they clear theirs up?

"I've also learned that children won't fold things up and put them in drawers. But they will put things in baskets especially if they're nice baskets. I love those picnic baskets with lids and have different ones for different things like dolls' clothes and socks. I label each one clearly so the girls know what goes in which. All they have to do then is pick up and drop. Even a four year old can do that because it's like a sorting game.

"The same goes with toys. Each child can have a basket with their own name on it, clearly labelled, in the lounge. At the end of the day, they put their own toys in their own basket. You can do the same with shoes by the front door.

"Another key word is repetition. Keep saying it. Put your toys in the basket. Put your shoes in the basket. Eventually it gets through. Also remind them that everything has a place and show them where that is.

"Praise and reward is another important phrase in our house. When the girls were little, we had a star chart and everyone was on it, even the dogs. At the end of the month, the winner got something really nice.

"Frankly, we've never had trouble with homework because the girls know that school would discipline them if they didn't do it.

"When I was a child, I did very little to be honest. It wasn't until I moved out to a place on my own, that I started to be tidy. Now when I go to my mother's house, I'll start tidying up. It makes her laugh. So the good news is that even if your children are messy now, there's plenty of time for them to change."

Key points

- *Now they're really getting to a stage where they can help out.* But make sure you thank them and know they're appreciated
- *Consider linking jobs to pocket money* if you haven't already. Decide which jobs should be paid for and which ones they should do anyway

- *Write jobs down on a noticeboard or list.* Children of this age have a lot to think about

- *Use jobs to develop their personalities* Fit the job to the child. Allow them to choose jobs. It might even lead to a skill or future job if they prove dab hands at cooking/ironing/tidying up

Chapter 4

How to get 12 to 18 year olds to do the things they hate

JOBS THEY CAN DO

Still short of ideas on how they could help? Here are some jobs they should be able to do.

Cleaning shoes

Give them their own shoe cleaning kit and show them how to use it. You can make one up cheaply with a shoe box and essentials inside. Or you can buy one of those sachets like moistened tissues which don't need much elbow grease. Set aside one day of the week and a time when everyone in the family cleans their shoes. Sunday night is a good one.

Definitely get them to do their own trainers. Teach them to knock them against each other (the shoes, not the kids), *outside* the house and not in, so all the dirt is outside.

Shopping

If you're worried about them going shopping on their own, or if their little hands can't cope with heavy bags, set them up on the computer and get them to do a home shop for you. Arm them with a list first so they more or less buy the right things. And always check what they've ordered before keying in your credit card details. We suggest you do the latter yourself otherwise they might just be tempted to use your card for other things.

Put it in the microwave

This is a job that any streetwise kid worth their salt should know how to perform. So next time they moan that they're hungry (even though you've just cooked them a four course meal), teach them to read the microwave instructions and press the right buttons.

Work the washing machine

And the tumble drier. Also check your guarantee in case they break it in the process. Teach them to empty the filter which is usually located at the bottom of the machine. Many an adult doesn't know how to do this until the repair man says 'Didn't you read the instruction booklet?'

Dishwasher

Don't just teach how to load it or put it on. Also explain how to put dishwasher powder in and salt.

Empty the vacuum cleaner

Preferably into the bin and not on the floor.

Move furniture to vacuum underneath

This one's for older children.

Read bedtime stories to younger children

Get them to enjoy it by putting on funny faces. Demonstrate first of all.

Help them to amuse younger children by:

- Putting on puppet shows
- Making puppets out of gloves
- Playing board games
- Playing hide and seek
- Dancing to music

WARNING *Never leave younger children in the care of older children unless an adult is nearby.*

Clean out kitchen cupboards

Demonstrate first. Tell them they might find something interesting. Ask if they will rearrange things such as tins in one place and packets in another.

Empty your bin

Give each of them their own bin for their bedrooms. Try a different colour for each child. Make one day a week the 'bin cleaning' day. Ideally, make it the same day as your dustmen come. Then get them to put out the family bin at the same time.

Wash the bath out

Give them a pinny and make it fun. Give them the right cleaning materials and don't expect a brilliant job. But it will be a start. Next time, you can start them on the taps. Show them how to wrap a flannel round them and give them a buff.

Tidy the linen cupboard

If necessary, just get them to do one shelf. It's better than nothing.

Top tip

One friend got her kids to design shelf labels on sticky labels, for example 'towels', 'sheets' and so on.

Dusting

Give them a bright feather duster to make it more fun.

Tidying up other people's bedrooms

Get them to sort out your own dressing table or bedroom. Other people's rooms are always more interesting than your own. But make sure you hide any incriminating evidence first.

Give each child a 'tidy tray' or drawer

Get them to put things in it that they come across – they can do this for others in the family too. Set aside a certain time every week for putting these things back in the right place.

Use the stairs

I have a friend who has taught her children to put stray items at the bottom of the stairs. Every time someone goes up, they take something and put it away.

WARNING *You can fall over stair items and break an ankle, so make sure they're stacked right by the edge.*

Go through your old make up/tool box/whatever

This involves a certain amount of trust as they might throw away things you really want. So check the rubbish bin after they've finished.

Under the bed

Isn't it funny how kids often love the things you hate? One of my worst jobs is crawling under the bed to vacuum, only to find things that have been left there for years. But ask the kids to clean under the bed and explain what a great opportunity it is to wriggle around in the dark, and they'll jump at it.

Top tip

Allow them to keep any 'finds' they come across like coins or other treasures.

Answering the telephone nicely

Even well brought up children can let you down on the phone with a 'Yes' or 'What?' when they pick up the receiver. This one can only be achieved through constant nagging and also – it has to be said – setting the right example. Try writing down an agreed phrase and getting them to repeat it, parrot fashion.

You could encourage them or give them practice by allowing them to record a message on the answer phone. But do make sure it's clear and to the point. What might seem cute to adoring parents can actually be very yuk to callers.

When they ring someone else, enforce the importance of not just saying 'Can I speak to Peter?' but talking to whichever adult picks up the phone first. I learned this the hard way when the mother of a boyfriend complained I treated her like a telephone operator. Ever since then, I have always made a point of making polite conversation with whoever picks up the phone. And I also try to get my kids to do the same.

...and taking messages

'Someone rang,' is a favourite message via my son. Not who – he often can't even remember if it's male or female – but someone. So leave a pad of paper by the phone; preferably one that's big enough for them to see with an extra large jumbo pen or pencil firmly attached. Divide into columns with a heading for the caller, one for the time of call, another for the message, and one for the caller's phone number. With any luck, you'll get at least one of them.

Pick up their bathroom towel

Otherwise they have a wet one the next day. And no, *don't* pick it up yourself.

Clearing away old newspapers

Do this the day before the refuse collectors come. Make it a routine and they should (one day, before they leave home) do it automatically.

Cleaning out the fridge

A great way of teaching them how to spot sell-by dates. You can also use the opportunity to explain basic food rules like not storing raw meat next to cooked meat. Then, with any luck, they'll remember how not to give themselves food poisoning when they move into a student house.

Cleaning the loo

Another one that will come in handy when they have homes of their own. Someone will thank you for it one day.

Tidy up

Give them funny folders to put stuff in.

Basic cooking

Teach them how to bake a potato, make an omelette, and so on.

WARNING *Also show them how to use a fire blanket/extinguisher.*

Turn out lights

Stick Post-it notes next to the switch, reminding them how much electricity costs.

Bring down mugs from their bedrooms

If/when they don't, refuse to make them another cup of tea or coffee until they comply.

Learn to drive

So they can do the school run.

Mix cocktails for guests

They'll love this one. Buy them a fancy mixing recipe book and let them get on with it. Of course, they'll have to taste it first of all, just to make sure they've got it right.

Make your bed as well as theirs

Tell them that as they've done theirs so well, they can do yours too.

WHAT TO DO IF THEY DON'T CO-OPERATE

This is where we get tough. Refuse to do things for them. If they won't clear the table or make the bed, you won't have time to drive them into town.

Explain that as a working parent, you need help

If you don't work outside the home, point out that a family needs to be run on team effort. Everyone has to do their bit.

Reduce their pocket money

Or you could tell them they can't go to that concert on Saturday night. You need to be a toughie for this and it does rather depend on how bolshie they've been. But consider it.

Try positive discipline

Fill a jam jar with one pound coins and tell them they can have the lot at the end of the week if they do all their jobs. Every time they refuse to do a job, take a pound out and put it in your own purse. You'll either end up with more spending power or compliant children. Either way, you win.

Top tip

I do this myself with my nearly 15 year old and it works like a treat. You must use a jam jar however, or a see-through container so they can see the cash. For some reason, it's an important incentive.

Shame them

You can do this by asking their friends what jobs they do round the house. Your child might then admit they do zilch. If you really want to put your child down, you can do it for them. Researching this book has definitely shamed my lot into doing more because I interviewed every one of their friends who visited.

Don't do any jobs for them

This idea was suggested by many parents who filled in our survey. If they won't make their bed, leave it unmade. If they won't clear their plate, leave it on the table. Sooner or later, the mess will force you to have a discussion (i.e. argument). It might just clear the air and get something done about it.

Give up

This idea was also suggested by some parents in our survey. We all do it from time to time. And there is a case for picking your battles and only making a fuss about certain jobs. On the other hand, if you let them get away with doing nothing, you're not helping them to become responsible adults.

IT WORKED FOR US! PARENTS' TIPS

"I didn't push my daughter to do much around the house when she was young. But when she got to 14 or 15, she automatically started helping. It just came naturally and I think that's better than nagging. It shows that sometimes it pays to wait until they're old enough to want to do it or understand why you need help. I also encourage them to do the jobs they like. My son is building a garden shed with his father at the moment and he likes that. My daughter really enjoys cooking. We concentrate on the positive. It's never too late."

Bev

"My two youngest are 14 and 15. They both cook a meal a week and clean the kitchen afterwards. This is to help their cooking skills and also to help me. I was one of those mums who made the first two start doing their own washing and ironing and cooking one meal a week when they were 15. My oldest son is now very grateful for the grounding it's given him. At other times, I make a list of all the jobs that need doing. Then we work as a team, crossing off each job as it's done. This way, it's seen as fair as the time spent is the same and the number of jobs doesn't count. When they were little, I used to get them to tidy their toys away by putting my hands in front of my eyes and counting to 10. Then when I uncovered my eyes, they froze. If they hadn't finished, I'd do it again – and I always acted flabbergasted that they could have done such a good job. I pretended to think they had used magic to tidy up. Ah for the days when fantasy was believable."

Elaine

"If your kids won't help, go on strike. It doesn't always work but they do learn to appreciate the things you do for them. No more washing, ironing, cooking, waking them for school, giving them lifts, giving them money. Let them cope for a month or two. It's murder and will reduce you to tears but once everything is back to normal, they appreciate the things they once took for granted."

Anon.

"We use a mixture of nagging, threatening to hide the Playstation and not allowing the 18 year old the use of the car. Sometimes, if things have got into a mess, my 13 year old son and I have weekend projects like having a blitz on all the bedrooms. He's also responsible for packing his own games kit three times a week. When he was little, he would tidy up shoes. He's meant to give me his lunchbox at the end of the day but sometimes, on Monday mornings, I find it all smelly at the bottom of his bag. I also have three older children and I was stricter with them about doing jobs. When you have only one left at home, you tend to do more for them because there isn't the pressure of family life. That's not always a good thing."

Maggie

"My two children, aged 11 and 14, don't do nearly as much as my sister's but they do make their beds, take out their rubbish from their bins and bring down their washing from their rooms. They are also very good at laying the table, helping in the garden and bringing me things if I ask them to. They do get pocket money at the end of each week (£3 each) but seem to be only too happy to help anyway. I think it could be because they are also at their father's house on Wednesday and Saturday nights and he is very strict."

Eileen

"My sister's children who are 15 and 18 do dishes (something she and I always did as children) and vacuum the house. They also wrap all the Christmas presents for her and peel potatoes. She pays them small amounts to do jobs. My stepson does the dishes at his mother's house and she pays him 70p a week."

Deborah

"Negotiate. But be prepared to find a different negotiating tactic every time."

Anne

"My children aged 13 and 15 clean the goldfish bowl every two months and make their own beds. They hate tidying their rooms even though I nag them. The best advice I can give is that they have to see a benefit to a job before they will do it willingly."

Pat

"My children are grown-up now so my memories are a bit vague. But I do know that the key is to start early. You can't say 'Now you're I3, I think it's time you started cleaning your room.' These routines have to be established very young and then they're never questioned."

Paul

"Keep pestering. Bargain as in, 'I'll do this for you if you do that for me'. Start early."

Gill

"My advice is to send them to their grandparents or better still, move out and bring the grandparents in. Our children, age 15, five and four are as good as gold for their grandparents. They do lots of jobs and know that it means they receive lots of presents. We also negotiate, negotiate, negotiate to get jobs done."

Anon

"My kids have left home but when they were younger, I found the sheer effort of getting them to do anything was more effort than it was worth, especially with boys. My daughter liked to cook and would sometimes clean the entire kitchen while I was out, as a treat. But most of them are resistant to anything that suggests it's 'their' job. Also, they have so much schoolwork that it seems harsh to put other things on them."

Liz

"I've paid my kids for years to do chores. I have fixed rates per job: vacuuming the house is £3; dusting £5; mowing the lawn £4. They do, however, get very low pocket money compared with their friends – £20 a month."

Jan

"I worked on the principle that if you want your shirt ironed/packed lunch made, then DIY."

Bernadine

"The trick is to start them young, make it fun and as they get older, make them think it's a privilege to be allowed to do certain things. When they get to their early teens, explain how tired you get, especially if you work, and tell them that for the sake of your health and the protection of their lifestyle, it's important that all family members play their part."

Margaret Morrissey, spokesman for the Parents Teachers Association

"This is what helps us with our boys, aged 15 and 17. Compromising. Showing how much you appreciate their help when they turn their hand to something. Letting them know you really need a hand, particularly if you are to have enough time to be able to give them lifts etc."

Sandra

"We have twins of 19 and an older daughter in her twenties. When the twins use the car, they have to clean it in return."

Sally

"I pay my 17 year old son to clean windows. But he does other jobs like getting the rubbish ready for collection day because it's expected of him. I persuade him through emotional blackmail, I'm afraid. For example, I might look tired and tearful. Sometimes I start to do it myself and he feels guilty and takes over. However, I don't think it's easy for children to help out round the house as they have so much homework. When my eldest daughter turned 16, I told her I would no longer iron her clothes as she was old enough to be responsible. But what happened? She didn't iron them at all and wore all her clothes crumpled and creased until I eventually gave in after six months."

Alison

"Our children, aged 14 and 12, get £7 a week if they clean the kitchen every day. They're expected to do their bedrooms for nothing. They also have to do their own washing if their clothes aren't in the basket on Friday night. We also agreed that a task should be time limited so they didn't feel too daunted."

Fiona

"We get our children aged 14 and 16 to do jobs by paying them a small amount, depending on the task, or imposing some sort of ban on the computer or television or Playstation. If they really won't do something, we might ban it all together, depending on the circumstances. Actually, I think my children probably help more than most, according to what they tell me. It's important to value your children and be positive about the things they do, especially the things they do well. This builds up confidence. We all have to do things we hate and it's best to help children to understand this at an early age."

Sheila

"We have three children, aged 14, 13 and nine. When we're together, we discuss chores and see how we can make things easier on everyone. It's like a group family meeting but not so formal."

Victoria

"My 12 year old son tidies his bedroom under duress, loads the dishwasher, takes rubbish out when asked, makes the odd cup of tea and occasionally helps me with paperwork like addressing envelopes, sorting receipts into piles and doing some filing. I nag to get the tidying done and pay for things like office filing or sweeping up leaves. I also threaten him with my not helping *him* next time he asks. Or I say he can't go somewhere/watch Eastenders. A friend of mine takes the controller for the Playstation and television away. I've tried this and it's very effective. However, I also think it depends on how many children you have. My son is an only so I have got used to doing too much for him. If I had four of them, they would have to do more. I also bore him rigid by telling him, in an old bag voice, about all the things I had to do as a child. I explain that life is full of having to do things you don't want to do and that this is good training for when they have to go out to work and have horrid kids of their own. With any luck, he goes off and does the jobs he should do just to get away from me. The ultimate threat is that I tell my son that if he won't do a job with good grace, I will turn up at his school, wearing flowery jeans and lots of lipstick, call him 'my little soldier' and kiss him in front of all his mates."

Jane

"Instead of threatening to limit their television time if they don't do jobs, we give them extra television time when they *do* do them."

Anon

"Our 15 year old puts washing in the washing machine and tumble drier. I also take away Playstations, iPods and television in his room as a sanction. And I look very disappointed if something isn't done."

Anon

"We don't have to nag our 13 and 15 year olds because they learned the habit of doing jobs round the house from a young age. They do things like tidying their bedrooms, washing up, loading the dishwasher and making their beds as soon as they get home from school. It's the norm for them."

Suzanne

"My 13 year old son does the vacuuming as his main 'pocket money' chore. He actually enjoys dusting and started at about five because he used to enjoy spraying the cleaning products. I've tried to encourage him to tidy his room from an early age but my own isn't very tidy so that's a hard one to set an example for. However, he hates the washing up. So if I need to discipline him, instead of grounding him, I get him to do the pots every night for a week. Sometimes I give him the old 'We're a team' spiel. I'll also tell him he's not allowed to go out with his friends until the job has been done. I think you need to let go, as they get older, rather than mollycoddle them. Shut the door on their room if you can't stand the mess. It's their space and as long as they help to keep the communal space tidy, don't nag. Once they're older and able to take care of their own chores, don't do it for them. Let them go out scruffy and as soon as their friends start poking fun at them, they'll learn."

Andrea

"Our children, aged 11 and 16, wash and dry up, load the dishwasher, iron, help with younger children, take out the milk bottles and cook. We waited until they were 10 before we got them to do jobs but then we persuaded them by paying them for big jobs like ironing. They can also be encouraged to cook if they take care of the whole project, like doing the shopping and planning. Parents often let children get away with not doing jobs round the house because they don't have enough time to stick to their guns. We also try to make jobs fun and when we're on holiday, we all do the washing up together."

Katy

"I find that a list or rota is useful to remind both me and them that certain tasks should be delegated. I've also found that sending children to boarding school makes them much lazier as everything is done for them. One of their biggest faults is leaving towels on the bathroom floor as at school there's underfloor heating. Ouch!"

Nicki

"My kids are in their twenties now but when they were teens, the best way to get them to do jobs they hated was to beg."

Anon

Novelist and mother Katie Fforde says: "I feel I was hopeless in this department but now they're in their twenties, they're fine at doing chores. So it shows all is not lost..."

Key points

- *Your kids are growing up* They need to do jobs at home to prepare themselves for the wide world and university
- *So if you let them off* you're not doing them any favours
- *Encourage team work* if you've got more than one child
- *Show them the benefits of helping out* e.g. being able to find their homework easily

Chapter five

Tidy your room!

Well, after all, this is what the book is about. The funny thing about tidying up is that we expect ourselves and others to be able to do it automatically, a bit like breathing. No one sits down and tells us how to do it. There aren't any lessons like there are for reading or driving or any other skills.

So although it might sound a bit simplistic and possibly patronising, this chapter is about how to tidy up and how to impart these skills to your children, however old they are. Some of the following sections will apply to younger children as well as older ones. But often it depends on your child's ability and willingness. So instead of dividing them into ages, we've divided them into strategies and tactics.

When you're explaining how to tidy up, do the job yourself first of all, talking about what you're doing while your children watch. After that, you can do the job together. Then your children can do the job on their own while you watch and encourage them and gently explain how they might do something differently. And then your children can do it on their own.

IN THE BAG

Tell them to start with the floor. Get down on your hands and knees with them and start picking up any rubbish. If their room is like my son's, you'll find old crisp packets, tin rings, loose chains and lost homework in all kinds of unexpected places.

If necessary change the bag. Don't say 'Look at all this rubbish. Aren't you awful.' Try 'That's fantastic. We've got one bag full and now we're going onto another.'

You'll be amazed at the results. Simply tidying the floor will give an instant feeling of space and, dare we say it, tidiness.

Take another bag and tell your kids that this one is for things that they don't want to throw away but need to put in a different place. When the bag is full, go through each item in the bag and find a place for it. For example, if it's a lost sock, put it in the sock basket or drawer.

ON THE SURFACE

Then move on to surfaces. Put rubbish into the bags from the top of desks, units, beds and so on.

DIVIDE IT UP

If your kids have a big room or there's a huge amount of mess, we suggest you divide the room up into quarters. This can actually be a good mathematical exercise. Help them tackle one quarter of the room one day and another the next and so on. You can use furniture in the room to help you make the divisions. For example, say 'We'll do this side of the bed today and that side tomorrow.'

Alternatively, you could do the floor one day and the surfaces on another.

WIPE IT UP

Now they've moved all that rubbish from their desk or dressing table or whatever, it might be a bit mucky underneath. Give them a damp cloth and show them how to rub off ring stains etc. Then find them a duster and polish. Don't just say 'Dust' but show them how to spray enough polish and not too much. Make a game out of rubbing the duster in different movements.

If you're feeling really strict or you want to get your kids truly house trained, show them how to wipe down skirting boards with the cloth. This might sound obvious to us but it won't be to them and sometimes it's worth remembering that.

SWEEP IT UP

Show your children how to use the vacuum cleaner. Obvious? Not always. My then 13 year old son almost managed to decapitate my vacuum cleaner and if it hadn't been for the lovely woman on the other end of the phone at Customer Services, I would have been distraught.

Also show them how to use the dustpan and brush. This is a much forgotten item but is very easy for young children to use. If they can be trusted on the stairs, show them how to kneel on the top step, sweep it and then go down one step at a time.

PUT IT IN ITS PLACE

One reason why rooms get so untidy is that children don't know where to put things. So make sure everything has its place in life. Socks go in the third drawer down. Books go on the table by the bed or on the bookshelf. CDs go in the rack.

- This might mean buying containers or other things to store these items in. But that doesn't have to be expensive. Shop around for inexpensive plastic crates and label them so everyone knows what's inside.
- Keep shoe boxes when buying new shoes and store the shoes in these. It's cheaper than those shoe tidiers.

- Also hang on to old containers for storing things. Pringle tubes make great containers for rubbers and pencils.

EASY TO GET TO

Children are more likely to put things in their right place if that place is easy to get to. It's unrealistic and dangerous to expect a small child to reach up to a top drawer or one that is always sticking. In fact, any kind of effort – such as finding the right drawer – can be enough to put them off the task altogether. So try open baskets where they can see at a glance what's inside.

- Hanging rails can also be handy because children can see what's there at a glance. But make sure they're not too high for them to reach. And only buy sturdy makes which won't fall over on your child.
- Save ice cream containers for storing hair scrunches, loose coins, paper clips, bits of Lego etc. Use sticky labels to put on the lid so you know what's inside.
- Buy see-through plastic envelopes or folders for important information that they want to keep themselves.
- Put a noticeboard on their wall so they can pin up notices and any other bits of paper which they want to keep safely.
- Get a blackboard or whiteboard and prop it against their wall. They can use it to write things down so they don't forget. And you can use it to remind them of what they're meant to be doing when you say 'tidy up'.

COLOUR CO-ORDINATE

Grouping clothes together according to colour isn't just an adult thing. It also makes it easier to find children's clothes. And it makes it easier for them to put away a pink jumper or a blue one because they know where they go.

We also have a separate drawer for sports kit which, in theory, saves us from looking in different places for football shirts, socks etc.

DO YOU REALLY, REALLY WANT THIS?

Decluttering is becoming increasingly popular for adults. And amazingly, kids can feel better too when they get rid of their rubbish. Go through their wardrobe and drawers and anything else and ask if they still want something. Get them to try on clothes and see if they still fit. At the rate kids grow, you'll be amazed at how much storage space you're giving to stuff that doesn't even fit any more.

Bag it all up and get them to help you take it to the charity shop or friends whose children will still enjoy it. My kids get a lot of pleasure out of this. Recently, we gave some things to a neighbour's son who wrote us a thank you letter. I thought that was lovely – and surprisingly, my children were touched too.

Key points

- *Tidying up* is a skill that often needs to be taught. Don't assume they know what to do when you tell them to sort out their room or school bag.
- *Go through each stage* Show them how to do it even if it seems obvious.
- *Make sure* there's a place and home for every major item in your child's room so they know where it goes.

Chapter six

Kids' backchat

Of course, to find out what *really* makes kids do the jobs they hate, who better to ask than the culprits themselves? We spent several months researching the answers. With the teenagers, we had to wait until the morning after the night before, in order to get a sensible answer.

"I cook, clean, wash clothes, vacuum, do the dishes, load and unload the dishwasher, drown squirrels (sic), tidy my room, garden, iron, make beds, clean bins, water plants. My mum's a slave driver."

James, 19

"I do the dishes, tidy my room and wash the car. We just do it."

Andrew, 19

"I tidy my room, do the dishes and help garden. I have to."

James, 19

"I vacuum and can even change the hoover bag. I taught myself, I think. I learned to vacuum when I was about nine because I was made to for pocket money. I definitely hoover round corners although they're the most annoying things to do. I wash up and dry up without being asked because otherwise my mum would ask me so it's better to get it out of the way before she nags me. We're redecorating at the moment so I paint and strip walls. I'm quite good at taking the paint off windows. My mum taught me how to do this. In return, I get paid money which goes into the rugby tour fund; I'm hoping to go with school later this year. I can do washing as well. I can put it in the machine on the right number, depending on what clothes they are, and put in detergent. I've never shrunk anything. I do so much because my mum makes me."

Kieran, 15

"I walk the dog all the time. I got a dog when I was 13 so I knew not to cross the road at dangerous times. I also give the dog a bath sometimes but he hates it. I do vacuuming sometimes when I'm asked. I haven't broken the vacuum cleaner yet but my mum has. I can change the bag; it's quite easy because it's a clip on. I mow the lawn but it's hard because it's on a hill. I don't have to be nagged but I do it when I need money and my parents realise the house needs cleaning. I don't really tidy my room because I share it with my brother and he messes it up so there's not much point. I also wash the family car about once a month. I get extra money for that – about £10 depending on how well I wash it."

Matt, 15

"I clean the car when I'm desperate for money. I get £10 max if I do a good job. I hoover round the house occasionally if my mum really nags me. I sometimes use my dad's sit-on mower. I like doing this and he pays me £5 if I mow the lawn. Occasionally I tidy my room if my mum nags me a lot. I lay the table when my mum is cooking for me. I put all my own stuff in the dishwasher when I've finished. I've hung out the washing for my mum in the summer. I sometimes cook breakfast in the morning. My mum taught me how to make scrambled egg."

Will, 15

"Bribery is the only thing that works. Just give us money."

William, 22 (author's son)

"We've always had to make our beds and tidy our bedrooms. My mum writes a list of jobs and puts our name down next to them, like emptying the dishwasher and vacuuming and doing the ironing –

that kind of thing. If you don't do it, she gets pretty stressed out and you get shouted at. We water the garden and do the chemicals for the swimming pool as well as vacuuming it and putting the pool covers on at night. We rake the leaves in the autumn and mow the lawn. I've made dinner for everyone every night since I was 11. My friend says I make great quiches. As I got older, my younger brother Sam would help me do pasta. We have a cleaner who comes in twice a week as well so there isn't that much to do. But we would always wash up after dinner before dad gets back from work. When my brother and I were in the same class at school, I'd have to help him with his homework."

Laura, 19

"I wash up and dry up and do a bit of ironing. I also tidy up and stuff. Round mealtimes, I help in the house. I also do loads of gardening for my mum; digging the vegetable garden and walking the dogs every day. Mum tells me to do this. She used to pay me for doing the car but that stopped because I stopped washing the car. I got bored with it. If I don't do the jobs mum asks me to do, she throws a tantrum."

Sam, 15

"I don't hate doing any jobs. I just can't be arsed to do them. Also, we weren't brought up having to do jobs, so we don't do them. The best way to get us to do jobs is to treat us like adults. Don't nag or get cross or make us feel guilty if we don't do it. Then we will do it, if you see what I mean."

Charlie, 14

"I tidy out kitchen cupboards for mum. I like it because I put all the pots and pans inside each other."

Mary, eight

"I like using the vacuum cleaner because it makes me feel grown-up."

Lizzie, seven

"I hate tidying my room but mum gives me a Tesco bag on Sunday nights and makes me pick up rubbish from the floor. I get 30p a bag."

Matthew, nine

"My mum can't see very well so my five brothers and I all have different jobs. My job is to put all the newspapers in a pile by the back door and then one of my brothers puts the bin out."

Jason, five

"My dad's always moaning that he doesn't have time to watch television since mum went. So I thought of circling the programmes I think he'd like in the paper and getting him to sit down sometimes. He says it's my new job."

Melissa, 10

"I put knives and forks on the table before meals. Sometimes I put them the wrong way round."

Kerry, five

"I like making paper decorations for the table when it's Christmas or someone's birthday."

Susan, six

"I like vacuuming mum's cutlery drawers with the end of the vacuum cleaner. I take all the knives and forks and spoons out first and then get the mess out. It's amazing what you find. Bits of dirt, crumbs and fluff. I'm always telling her she should be tidier. When I have my own home, it's not going to be like this."

Andrea, 12

"My job is to put my shoes and my younger brother's shoes in a tidy row every Sunday night in the hall."

Mandie, six

Chapter seven

What the experts say

If we really want to get kids to do jobs they hate, we need to employ some psychological cunning. And sometimes, as we parents know all too well, it's time to call in the professionals. We asked experts who are parents too, for some tips and general advice.

WORK OUT WHAT KIND OF JOB YOU WANT THEM TO DO

"There are two types of jobs," says psychologist and mother Gaynor Sbuttoni. "One is the kind of job your child needs to do to help himself. And the other is the kind of job your child can do to help others.

"The trick is to concentrate on the first and work up to the second. If you can help your child to learn to make his own bed, or pack her homework for the next day, or empty their own wastepaper bin, you are teaching them to be self-sufficient. When they've mastered that, it's nice to get them to help others so they learn how good that feels."

DON'T BE VAGUE – BE SPECIFIC

Don't just say 'tidy your room' or 'clear up your toys', says Gaynor. "With my children, I've found it's essential to talk them through the basic stages such as where to put the toys or what to do with those magazines that are lying on the floor. Sometimes a job seems so vast and overwhelming that they don't know where to start and that's when they give up. But if you've given them definite instructions, they know what they're doing and they're more likely to do it."

Editor's note – see chapter 5.

BIN IT

Penny Palmano, writer, mother, stepmother and author of *Yes, Please. Whatever! (Thorsons Element £7.99)*, has also solved the 'Put away your clothes' problem by buying her children a big plastic bin each for them to chuck clean clothes into. "When I just told them to hang up their clothes, they either did it sloppily or not at all." Bins are easy and also specific which is what this section is about. If you say 'Put it in the bin', that's pretty clear. And as Penny says, it's better than clothes lying on the floor. "The other great thing is that they don't have to fold them. I also give them plastic trays to put their make up on."

Top tip

Buy storage containers or baskets for young children to put away their toys.

ROLE MODELLING

"Show them how to do things by getting down on your hands and knees (if necessary) and demonstrating," says Gaynor. "So if they are having trouble tidying their room, show them how you tidy the kitchen and get them to help you. Say 'You do that bit there and I'll do this and we'll see what we're left with'."

Gaynor suggests talking out loud while you're doing this to encourage them and to give them ideas. "Try something like 'Oh dear, I need to find a new place for this. Now let's see, where can it go'. Then they can think about whether they would do the same to their bedroom."

Penny Palmano agrees. "Don't just say 'Please can you vacuum the carpet'. Explain how to go into corners. And show them how the different attachments to the vacuum cleaner go on and off."

"In fact, explaining how to do something is crucial," adds Dr Pat Spungin, psychologist, mother and founder of **www.raisingkids.co.uk**. "Otherwise it can stop children wanting to do it again if they get it wrong – and cause family arguments. My husband once offered one of our daughters money to paint the garden furniture. But he didn't explain how to do it and she got paint all over the patio."

WHAT TO DO IF THEY WON'T CO-OPERATE

Keep reminding them

This tip is from me. Unless your child is a natural home maker (and there are a few which we'll come onto later), you'll need to remind, remind, remind. In fact, there's nothing wrong with reminding them to do something, so don't start berating your kids for never listening. It takes time for the tidying up gene to kick in – especially if you've started a little late in their lives.

However, it is a bit boring to be the baddy reminder, so here are some things that might help them remember for themselves.

- *Make a checklist of jobs they have to do* Write out a small list of tasks and get them to tick them off when they've finished. Don't put too many on the sheet or they'll feel overwhelmed. Just seeing it written down, will jolt their memory and remind them. Put the list somewhere they will see it. Try anywhere near their computer/music/mobile for starters. Or stick it to the back of their bedroom door so that when they slam it after a row with you, they'll see what they really should be doing.

- *Tie it into a day* If it's Tuesday, it must be the day to empty bedroom wastepaper bins. Mark it on the kitchen calendar. Then say something like 'It's Tuesday. What do we do on Tuesdays?'

(*Warning:* We can't accept responsibility for inappropriate answers)

- *Have house rules which are set in stone* "Draw up a list of house rules which includes jobs that certain people have agreed to do," suggests Dorit Braun, chief executive of ParentLine Plus. "It might be things like putting your dirty washing in the bin – and if you don't, it won't get washed".

Write it down

"I wrote out a code of behaviour for my son and gave it to him," says Heather Summers, communications and language expert and the author of *The Book of Luck, (John Wiley £12.99).* "It included being polite and saying things like 'Good morning' and 'Good night'. Sometimes teenagers need things to be written down to make it go in."

Start young

This tip was repeated again and again by all the experts we asked. So if you've just had a new baby, it's time to read this. Within a year, you'll be able to send your newborn off to work. Only half joking. "Even toddlers can pull up their own duvet in the morning," says Dr Pat Spungin. "The sooner you start, the more used they will be to helping round the house or doing things for you. They won't question; they'll just get on with it."

Penny Palmano points out that the great thing about young children is that they actually think it's fun to help clean up the kitchen and dust. "Give toddlers their own special cleaning box with their name on it. Don't ask if they will do something. Tell them but in a nice way. 'Today, we're going to wipe down the cupboards in the kitchen.'"

Sue Firth, a psychologist, is a great believer in the starting young theory. "My seven year old daughter does jobs like clearing up her own toys. I've taught her that if she gets something out, she has to put it back. To get them going, I also advise finding a job your child enjoys and then working on it. My daughter loves setting the table and playing 'waitresses'. Recently, she's started to take our orders, which can be a bit annoying after a while but we go along with it. My son likes tidying up the playroom. We also link jobs with pocket money. Georgina, who's seven, gets £3 a week and Ben, five, gets £2.

"Ben also enjoys doing the polishing and I give him his own pinny and duster. I try not to be controlling and I don't point out the bits he's missed. Sometimes I say 'Here are the top five jobs for the day. Which ones would you like to do?' Then they pick one and can earn extra pocket money."

But it's never too late

If you've allowed your teenager to get away with it, you can still get him or her to make a start. Use a birthday as a starting point. 'Now you're 15, you can cook and clear away a meal.' Or 'Now you're 11, you can wash the basins.'

Top Tip

"I find it hard to clean my bathroom because I'm arthritic," says Granny B from Buckinghamshire. "So I suggested to my 12 year old grandson that he does all the 'white stuff' in the bathroom, including the toilet, for £10 a week. He comes on Saturday mornings and afterwards we have a cup of tea together. I make sure he washes his hands first."

Turn it up

This is another of my own tips. Jobs don't have to be done in silence. Put on the radio. It will take away the tension. If they're tidying their own bedrooms, suggest they put on some of their terrible music. I actually dance with one of my children when we're doing the housework together. I won't tell you which one because it will embarrass them. But it's fun and it makes us laugh instead of getting tetchy.

You help me and I'll help you

A tit for tat – in the nicest possible way – can work wonders when it comes to getting kids to do things they hate, says Gaynor. "'If you help me set the video timer, I'll help you tidy your wardrobe.' It helps them feel valued. Often kids are the ones who feel thick or inadequate because an adult is always telling them they are doing something the wrong way. But if they've got talents that the adult hasn't got, it makes them feel great about themselves. And it also shows them the pleasure of helping others. Presenting a job as part of a bargain makes them see the sense of doing jobs. Children are usually very fair underneath. They can see that if someone does you a favour, it needs to be returned."

Penny Palmano agrees. "Next time your teenager wants a lift, agree – providing he does something for you so you have time to give him that lift. It might be tidying your home office or washing up."

Bribery

Should you or shouldn't you bribe your kids to do jobs? The experts and parents we interviewed were divided on this one. After all, if your kids expect something every time they do something for you, where do you stop? But our experts also had some other interesting ideas.

- *If you are going to bribe them* keep rewards small, advises Gaynor. Or you lose the value of rewards for something more important. Children also need to learn that it's nice to do jobs to help others and not just to earn money.

- *Keep the rewards in perspective* advises Dr Spungin. "Don't promise them a fortnight's holiday if they keep their room tidy for ever. Be realistic. Make sure the reward is attainable and that it's not overindulgent".

- *Link pocket money to certain jobs*, says Penny Palmano. "There's a time when this can definitely get them going. After all, it's earning money for fair labour. We pay cash if it's a really tricky job like gardening. They get £4 an hour for weeding or cleaning the car. But be careful not to do this with all jobs or they'll expect cash in hand for everything."

- *Employ them like you would a cleaning lady*, suggests Masha Bell, teacher, mother, grandmother and writer. "When my daughter got to the age of 14, I employed her as my cleaning lady. She wanted to get an outside job to earn money but it would have interfered with her interest in music. So I paid her the going rate as a cleaner and she did the house for me three hours a week. She took it seriously because we both saw it as a real job."

Professor Cary Cooper, expert in time management says "In my view, the only thing that works is bribery, otherwise known as 'incentive based parenting'. We already gave them an allowance but if we promised them extra, they did things. One thing I did learn was to ask them to do jobs on a Friday. They were so keen to earn money for going out at the weekend with their friends, that they were more likely to agree".

Top Tip

Paying by the hour also helps them get into a 'work' frame of mind for when they do holiday jobs or the real thing. It also shows them that an hour can be a long time to do something boring. So when they do go into the real world of work, they need to do something interesting. That can be an incentive for passing exams.

- *Show them how to earn money for jobs.* What's that old saying about there being plenty of money to be made out of rubbish? One of my children's friends, who's only 12, cleans out his room twice a year and sells the things he doesn't want on eBay using his older brother's account. He also goes down with his mother to the local car boot fair and sells other discarded items there. Last year, he made enough to buy a new computer.

- *Offer them an on-the-spot reward for the job.* As one parent says, "If I ask one of my teenagers to get some shopping for me in town, I'll give them some extra money to buy a pie at the baker's to make the walk home more interesting".

Praise them

We all know that no one does a job better than we can do ourselves, but if you say as much, you're not likely to get more help from that quarter. "Never say 'That's awful – call that tidying your room?'" says Penny Palmano. "Or they won't want to do it again. Give them plenty of praise. Say 'that's *such* a help' even if it hasn't been. Tell them how grown-up they are. After that, you can say 'Another way of tidying your room might be to pick up the towels that are still lying in the corner'. Don't yell if they put on so much furniture polish that it creates scum on top of the table. Instead, show them how to do it properly. Be positive about the things they haven't done, instead of being negative."

Encourage team work

Office psychologists know what they're talking about when it comes to encouraging team work. If we all feel we're working towards one cause, we might be more likely to enter into the spirit. "If you've got more than one child, get them to work as a team," advises Penny who has a 17 year old son, a 17 year old stepdaughter and an 18 year old daughter at home. "They often do jobs together like cleaning the kitchen. It's also nice because it gives them time to chat about things they might not otherwise have had time to talk about."

Dr Pat Spungin agrees. "Get your family to see themselves as a team. You can do this by encouraging everyone to pitch in. Don't assume you have to do it all yourself or they'll take the same attitude."

Top Tips

- Like Penny, I get my kids to do jobs together but I listen in to their chat. You can learn all kinds of things this way.
- Use peer pressure to your advantage. Show younger children how helpful older children can be; these might be siblings or neighbours' children etc. It gives them a goal to work towards.

Work with distractions

"If your children find it boring to do jobs round the house, let them do jobs in front of the television," says Penny. "My stepdaughter likes sorting odd socks this way. And small children can do the same with boxes of toys. That's why so many people do the ironing or use an exercise bike in front of the screen."

Top Tips

- "My children like polishing/vacuuming etc. when they have their iPods in. If they don't own an iPod, tell them that they need to do more jobs round the house to earn one. (See section on bribery.)
- "Get them to make a party out of a job. If they moan about washing up, set up the radio in the kitchen and get them all doing it. Young children, in particular, love this," says Dr Pat Spungin.

If you can't beat them

If you can't beat them, join them, says Penny. "Do jobs with them and use the time to share confidences. If you're both cleaning the kitchen, it's a great opportunity for some deep, meaningful chat. Changing the duvet cover in tandem is another example."

Appeal to their better natures....

"Tell them you could really do with some help because you're running out of time," says Penny. "This attitude works much better than

'You're so lazy; you never do anything for me.'" Penny also admits that the odd bit of emotional blackmail can come in handy. "If my lot are reluctant to walk the dog, I'll point out that he could be ill/have an accident/will have to live somewhere else unless they pull their weight."

Writer Masha Bell goes one further. "Don't be afraid to show them how you feel. If I was tired, I'd get cross and they'd usually respond to reason."

And don't let them get away with it

"When you come home from work and your big teenager is sprawled out over the sofa, asking what's for dinner, say 'Hang on a minute…,'" advises Dr Pat Spungin. "Once you start saying 'All right, don't you get up; I'll do it,' you're in trouble because they'll think they can get away with it next time too. However, it's worth picking your fights and deciding what you're going to get tough over and what you can afford to let slip. You can't win every argument so it's more important to fight for the ones which mean most. We personally have a rule that they help to tidy public spaces that everyone uses like the kitchen and sitting room. How they keep their own room is their own business. Compromise is also important. If they're really busy with their homework, let them off the washing up that night. Say 'I'll do it for you' but make sure they know it's still their job."

Let them get adventurous

Allow them to do jobs they might make a mess off – within reason. "Our teenagers have been ironing for years," says Penny. "But I don't give them my husband's shirts to iron. Instead, they've ruined their own t-shirts by ironing the motif. But if they don't make mistakes, they don't learn."

Dr Pat Spungin warns that we shouldn't assume our children are too young to do something. "A time always comes in a child's life when they are old enough to be taught how to operate the digital camera/washing machine/house alarm/answer phone. In fact, children are often better at technical things like digital cameras than adults because they're not frightened of them."

Top Tip

I know one mum who allowed her eight and 10 year olds to paint their own bedrooms. The effect was interesting.

Find them jobs that develop their creative instincts

"When my son was about 13, he filed our extensive collection of CDs and really enjoyed it because it appealed to his kind of brain," says Dr Pat Spungin. "Some children naturally enjoy ordering things – so they could sort out cookery books too. If they make a face when you ask them to peel vegetables, get a fancy shaped cutter. They might enjoy making a picture out of the food."

Life coach Jackie Arnold says "My children enjoyed gardening if they could do something creative like making up their own pots of plants."

Ask them nicely

No one likes being told what to do and even if you think your children *should* do something, they're more likely to respond if you ask them nicely, says Penny.

This also applies in front of outsiders. "If visitors arrive, don't automatically expect your children to take their coats or make polite conversation. Talk to them beforehand and discuss how they could help you."

Heather Summers suggests using your voice to get what you want. "Sound firm and go down in tone at the end, in a command. Don't shout. Use positive language. Instead of saying 'Your room is a mess,' try 'You know your bedroom needs tidying and today's the day for doing it so will you do it now.'"

Teach them skills that they'll remember for ever

Cooking is an obvious one, says Penny. "But keep it simple like how to warm up pasta sauce. If it's too complicated, they might switch off or think they can't do it."

Other skills could include:

- *Ironing*
- *Making beds properly* e.g. tucking in the corners
- *Putting on a duvet*
- *Peeling potatoes*

Top Tip

To change the duvet cover, turn it inside out and, while still holding the two top corners, grab hold of the two top corners of the duvet. Invert, rather like tipping out a steam pudding, and shake the duvet cover down. My friend's son learned to do this at boarding school and has been teaching the rest of us.

Your child's personality will dictate what jobs they will and won't do

"Certain ten year olds are capable of loading the dishwasher correctly and others aren't," reminds Masha Bell. "We need to accept their limitations. Tidying up was a problem for my son. Sometimes there's not a lot you can do to change them. But there may be other jobs that they are good at and other children aren't. The trick is to experiment until you find their niche."

Life coach Jackie Arnold agrees. "My children weren't good at tidying up. I also used to nag them to polish but they wouldn't do that either. However, they *did* enjoy ironing because they could see the results. Psychologically, for them, seeing the results is really important. You don't always get that when you tidy a room because it gets untidied fast. But an ironed shirt is proof that you've done something. Other children might be different. It's like nagging. Some respond to it and others don't. I've also learned the hard way that some children are more willing to do jobs than others. It depends on their personality. And there's not a lot you can do to change it."

Professor Cary Cooper suggests linking the job with your child's personality. "My son liked being praised. So if you've got a kid like that, give them a task they can do well and then tell them what a great job they've done."

"My son worked best when he had a choice of jobs," says Heather Summers. "I'd say 'Would you like to empty the dishwasher or cook breakfast?'. Creating a regular pattern of jobs also helps. He would empty the bins every Tuesday and he would always clear up after himself. I started when he was 14 by saying 'This is the deal; these are the rules in this house.' At first, he wasn't very good at some jobs but I made sure I didn't criticise him too much."

Give them time

You might have to wait a few years but they'll get there in the end... "My kids never tidied their rooms – not even when they went to uni," confesses Professor Cary Cooper. "But when they started to own their own homes, they got much fussier. So there is light at the end of the tunnel even if you have to wait 30 years."

Key points

- *Be consistent* If you give them a job, make them stick at it. Otherwise, they lose privileges.
- *Praise them* This can be verbally, financially or both.
- *Be imaginative* when giving them jobs. You need to make them interested.
- *Some kids will be keener on helping out than others* If yours is a reluctant helper, try and find a job he likes.

Chapter eight

The best way to ask your kids in order to get results...and other strategies

We warned you there was some psychology involved in this. Well, you've got to be a bit devious, haven't you?

FAMILY DIY AND OTHER EMOTIONAL INTELLIGENCE TIPS

There are some jobs which help to bond a family – and some that make families fall out for ever. We'd rather concentrate on the former. If you have a kid that's *very* bad at doing jobs, set them up with a partner, even if that has to be you. Choose jobs that genuinely require two people such as folding sheets, putting on a duvet etc. It might just provide that kick up the proverbial that they need.

Don't be afraid to cry

Some children respond best to direct payment for specific jobs. Others react better to emotional blackmail. For example 'Can't you see how tired mummy is?' It sounds obvious but each child is different. You know what will motivate yours in other areas so apply the same logic to housework.

Shameful ways to make them help out

OK, so this isn't really ethical. Let's hope no one from the child protection agencies are reading this. But bitter experience with three lazy kids has taught me that the best way to make them help out is to shame them in front of their friends.

There are various ways of doing this.

You can wait until one of their mates comes round and then ask them to help clear the table/wash up/polish their shoes. When they moan and say 'Get a life, mum, I've got a friend round', you then ask the friend if they help out at home. With any luck, the reply will be in the affirmative. You then say to your child: 'Well if your friend helps out, I think you should do the same.'

If the reply happens to be in the negative, by the way, do not ask that child round to tea again. He/she clearly isn't a suitable friend for your offspring.

Alternatively, you could ask the friends to help. If you say 'Would you lot mind putting your dishes in the dishwasher/wiping the mats?', chances are that they will be so much in awe of you that they will. After all, you're not their mum so they'll do what you say.

If you're clever, you'll wait until your kids' friends come round, before getting them to tackle some really dastardly jobs such as digging the garden/cleaning out the rabbit.

Pretend you can't do it yourself

There's nothing like a little woman to bring out the maternal side in kids. So mothers who are really desperate (and deceitful) they could pretend you simply can't lift up something without their help. We're sure you can think of some other examples.

Fit the child to the job

Some of our experts have already touched on this but we feel it's so important that we're saying it again. Some kids (if they've got any character) prefer certain jobs to others. So foster that. If they're great at washing up, hand over the Fairy Liquid. If they loathe washing up but quite fancy the idea of grooming the dog, make that their job instead.

Playing consequences

This is one of those home truths that you can't instill into your children early enough. If they make a mess, they have to clear it up. If they want to cook, they have to wash up afterwards. If they want to play with their toys, they clear them away. And if they won't, they can't do it again.

Sometimes you have to be tough as a parent. Maybe that's why I'm such a lousy one but *you* can still try.

TIME IT RIGHT

Every good politician and parent knows that it's not *what* they say – it's when they say it.

Asking the children to do jobs they hate, can succeed or fail depending on your timing. If you demand that they empty the bins/tidy their rooms when they're deep in conversation on MSN or vacant eyed in front of the television, you're on a losing wicket. So here are some tips:

Wait until they aren't doing something important and then make your request.

- Speak slowly and clearly, pretending that you're talking to someone whose native language isn't English. This might sound condescending but it's not intended to be. It's merely that children don't usually listen to adults so the clearer you can be, the more chance you have of getting through.
- Sometimes it helps to pretend that these children are not your own. Now I know this sounds awful but if you close your eyes and imagine they're your neighbour's kids, you might speak more

pleasantly to them and then you'll probably get better results than if you yelled. Trust me. This one works.

- Another weird tip, which has been tried and tested in our house by yours truly, is to speak with your eyes closed. For some reason, this stops you getting uptight about the fact that the job in question hasn't been done. You seem to concentrate on the words more than the feelings that are racing round your head. As a result, you speak in a calmer fashion. Well, just give it a go.
- Never yell instructions up the stairs. They won't hear you or they'll pretend not to hear you. If they do, they'll say 'What did you say?' or just 'Wot'. Then you'll have to run up the stairs and repeat the whole thing all over again. By then, you'll be feeling impatient and you probably won't ask them nicely enough for them to agree.
- Use new beginnings as new excuse for making them do jobs that they didn't do before.

Here are some examples.

- New year. Let's make helping out one of your new resolutions.
- New term. New leaf. Let's see if we can get a better report.
- New school. As above.
- New house. Now you've got a new bedroom, I want you to keep it tidy. Now we're moving house, you can pack your own things and throw away the bits you don't want.
- New baby. Now you've got a new brother/sister, I'm going to need more help. You can show him/her how grown-up you are because you can vacuum etc.
- Say 'Now it's a new year/term etc, we're going to do x,y,z'.

Jobs for each occasion

Use timelines and/or special occasions during the year to think up new jobs or encourage them to do old ones. Here are some examples.

- Christmas. Ask them to help write or design cards/envelopes/place mats. If necessary bribe them or just tell them that if they don't, Santa won't pay his usual visit.
- Easter. Instead of organising an Easter hunt for them, get them to do one for you. Ask them to hide small eggs round the house for you to find them. The reward is that they can help themselves as you go. It will keep them quiet while they're thinking you're doing them a favour. They could also organise an Easter hunt for visiting children.
- Summer holiday. Put one of them in charge of the calculator if you're going abroad, and get them to work out the exchange rate. Fantastic for maths. Yours, not theirs.

IT'S NOT WHAT YOU ASK THEM TO DO – IT'S THE WAY YOU SAY IT

Getting kids to do things they hate is often a matter of asking them in the right way. After all, if someone barked at you and told you to make supper now, you'd be less likely to do so than if that person asked you nicely.

Here are some ideas to get you going.

- Look them in the face. Direct your questions to their eyes and if they're not listening, do something to attract their attention. If necessary, do something really embarrassing. It usually works. This looking in the face bit is vital. It doesn't work if you yell an instruction down the stairs or call it out. It's far too easy then for them to ignore it.

- Another child ploy is to answer 'Yes' if you're asking whether they're doing their chores. As any child knows, a 'Yes' when an adult is out of earshot/eyeshot is just a ploy to put off the evil deed. So track them down and check they are actually doing it.

- If looking at them in the face doesn't work, try using your voice in a different way. This doesn't mean yelling or shouting although you're perfectly justified in doing that sometimes. Instead, try saying the instruction in French or Japanese or a made up language. If you're not fluent enough, just put on a foreign accent. They'll understandably look at you with a 'What is mum up to now?' look but it will get their attention. Then you can jump in and tell them normally, just what it is that you want them to do.

- Whisper. This is an alternative to the above. Of course they might not hear you with all the din they're making, but a whisper can be far more effective than a yell just because it takes them by surprise.

- Talk in a silly voice. The Dalek one seems to go down well.

- Sing. The same logic (or lack of it) applies.

- Ask them to do something in a poem. This does mean you have to be reasonably good at making up poems or limericks. But here's an example. Feel free to plagiarise.

  There was a young lady from Weitz
  Whose room was not very nice.
  Tidy up, said her mum
  Or it won't be much fun
  When your bedroom's infested with mice.

- Remember your pleases and thank yous. We think we've said this somewhere else in the book but it doesn't do any harm to repeat it. If we don't thank our kids for doing something or ask them nicely, why should they bother?

AIDES MEMOIRES

Sometimes, they need a little prod to help them remember what they have promised to do. Just like asking them to do something, you need to remind them nicely in order to get the most out of them. So try:

- Lists
- Wall charts
- Text messages on mobile phones. I do this every Wednesday to remind my son to go to his guitar lesson.
- Nagging
- If it's Tuesday, it must be ....

WHO'S A BIG BOY THEN?

Make them feel grown-up with big jobs. Children are often keener to do jobs if it makes them feel grown-up. Try these out for size and make them responsible for :

- Checking the smoke alarm batteries
- Doing the checking last thing at night
- Cooking supper. This includes planning the meal and shopping for it as well as washing up.
- Turning off the television
- Setting the house alarm
- Setting alarm clocks
- Putting the clocks forward and backwards at the right time of year

FLATTERY, BARTERING AND OTHER RUSES

We all know how nice it is to be praised and how soul destroying it is to be criticised. But it's easy to forget that in the day-to-day grind of constant nagging when it comes to the kids.

You're far more likely to get them to do jobs they hate if you tell them how good they are at something. All right, so there's still egg all over the plate while they're drying it up but at least they're trying.

The trick is to find something they really are good at and then plug it for all you're worth. My daughter is very good at tidying up kitchen shelves.

If they're not good at something, lie. Suppose you've asked your toddler to put away his toys and he's only put two in the toy box. The rest lie strewn over the floor as a booby trap for any sober adult. Do you say 'Why didn't you do what I asked?' No of course you don't. Instead, you cross your fingers and say 'Gosh, you've done a fantastic job with some of those toys. Now can you help me put the rest of them in the toy box?'

Another ruse is to make them into monitors for different jobs. My children's schools don't seem to have a monitor system but when I was at school, we had monitors in charge of different things like cleaning the blackboard. So do the same with your own brood. Make one the washing up monitor. Another could be the tidying up monitor. And if you've only got one child, you'll have to be a monitor yourself.

BARTER

In the old days, if we wanted a loaf of bread, we might barter a jar of honey for it. It's not a bad idea. Use it to give your kids a history lesson and get them to do things for you at the same time. Yes of course you will give them a fiver to go out with their friends or buy that comic. But only if they do something for you in return such as wash the car.

The trick is to explain this quid pro quo tactic in a nice and not nasty way. It's also essential for both parties to stick to the agreement. If you fulfil your side of the agreement even when they don't fulfil theirs, why should they do it next time?

DOING JOBS FOR EACH OTHER

One of the reasons why it's good for kids to do things they hate, is not just to lighten our own daily lengthy list of jobs. It's also to teach them how to be caring. If you have more than one child, you can take this a step further and get them to do jobs for each other. Always ask them nicely however. My 19 year old daughter often complains that I just expect her to do something for her younger brother even though he does very little for her. (She actually expresses this in a far less polite way which I can't elaborate on since this is a family book.)

Here are some examples of things older children could do:

- Help younger ones with homework
- Assist them with tidying up
- Show them how to do things like wash up/clear their room
- Wash younger children's hair

Younger children could:

- Help fold washing for older children
- Help make beds/change duvets
- Help carry things in from the car

TIDY UP INTERESTING PLACES

If you had a choice between tidying your room and tidying the attic or spare room, which would you rather do?

It's no contest, is it? Tidying a place which isn't yours and which offers interesting possibilities is much more appealing. It can also be very helpful. We've just moved house and it took me weeks to sort through all the rubbish we'd accumulated over the years. My husband and I agreed we should have done this years ago – and not just because of moving.

Clearing the house of stuff you don't need is actually very cathartic – and gives you more room to live in afterwards. So get the kids going. Send them up into the attic (supervised) or into the spare room where you've stored things you couldn't be bothered to chuck. Get an older child in charge – maybe a cousin or pay a neighbour's child – and ask them to sort things out in piles. For example, clothes, games etc.

Invite older children to make piles such as one for charity, one to keep, or one to give to friends. Get them to come with you down to the charity shop. It might be an eye opener for them to see what other people need.

Even better, allow them to hold a garage sale or take them to a car boot sale. They can keep the proceeds but only if they've done their fair share of sorting out first.

Top tip

If you don't have an attic or spare room, send them under their beds or yours. There's bound to be some rubbish there that needs sorting out.

COMPETITION TIME

If your kids are like mine, there's plenty of hot competition between them plus a large dollop of sibling rivalry. So keep it going by seeing who can be the tidiest or do the most jobs. Here are some ideas:

- Who can bring down the biggest number of dirty mugs from their bedrooms without spilling the contents on the carpet?
- Who can finish the drying up first?
- Who can make their bed first?

You get the idea....

GIVE ME FIVE – OTHERWISE KNOWN AS THE THREE LINE WHIP

Tell them what you want them to do. When they quibble, tell them they can have five/10/15 minutes to finish what they're doing now and then they have to do whatever it is you want. You stand a better chance of succeeding if you give them notice.

WHY BOTHER?

Let's face it. Getting kids to do jobs they hate can be more trouble than the jobs themselves. 36 per cent of the parents we surveyed, said they let kids off jobs because they couldn't be bothered to push it.

Psychologically, it's good for them

"If you let them get away with it," says psychologist Gaynor Sbuttoni, "it's not teaching them anything in the long term. If anything, it's telling them that if they make enough fuss about something, they won't have to do it. And that's dangerous, especially when it comes to school work. Instead, make it part of the routine. Agree the list of jobs in advance. Say 'This is going to be your job. Every Wednesday, I expect you to empty your bedroom bin/tidy your school bag out etc.'"

American research shows that children who help to sort laundry, water plants and dust, exhibit high levels of self-esteem, commitment and responsibility according to a recent feature in *Junior* magazine.

Children also take pride in earning money for jobs. And, as we remember ourselves, they'll value things that they bought with their own wages. "Children need to do jobs to learn the value of hard work and also responsibility," says Dr Pat Spungin, founder of **www.raisingkids.co.uk**. "It will also help them to become responsible partners when they settle down."

Even if they get in your way…

We all know the saying about too many cooks. This applies to kids too. It's very tempting to ask them to get out if they're under your feet, even if they're trying to help. But if you do, how will they learn? My mother was a great cook but had a small kitchen. Understandably, she didn't like anyone else in it. The result? I'm still learning to cook, at my age…

…or don't do it your way

No one will ever do things the way you would do them yourself. So what are you? A control freak? Loosen up and let them do it even if their way isn't as good as yours. You might even learn a few tips.

Here are some more advantages to getting kids to do jobs round the house

- Encourages manual dexterity
- Shows you mean what you say
- Helps you work as a team. Kids learn to realise that a whole family has to contribute if it's going to run smoothly.
- Can bring you closer if you do jobs together
- Makes them independent
- Increases their self-esteem especially if you praise them
- Teaches them to be kind
- Prepares them for being part of a partnership if they ever get married/live with someone
- Children who earn money for jobs, learn financial responsibility.

So why do we give up?

One mum who filled in her survey said it was because parents don't want to fall out with their kids. We can understand that. But on the other hand, we can't give in just to have an easy life, can we?

Key points

- *Use psychology* to get them interested. Explain why it's in their interest to help you. Tell them you're tired and need help. Flatter them and tell them how good they are at doing something.
- *Don't be afraid to barter* It's how the rest of the world works. If they do something for you, you'll do something for them.
- *If they won't do it,* there have to be consequences.
- *You're not nagging* You're helping them to become responsible adults even if you lose your voice and sanity into the bargain.
- *Choose your timing carefully* Ask them to do something at the right time and in the right place.
- *Don't give up* It won't really lead to an easier life in the long run because you'll still be the only one putting out the bins. Besides, they need to learn to be self-sufficient adults. Just like us. (Only half joking.)

Chapter nine

Work, work, work

There are so many jobs that a kid could do, that it's hard to know where to start. We've given you some tasters but here are a few more things to think about.

PRACTICAL JOBS THEY'LL THANK YOU (ONE DAY) FOR TEACHING THEM

How often have you wished you'd learned something a little earlier in life? Maybe you've blamed your own parents for not teaching you how to do something. Well, now's the time to take responsibility for passing that lesson on. There are certain practical jobs that all adults need to know. And they can start learning them when they're still kids.

Changing a light bulb

But teach them to check the electricity is off first.

Showing them where the fuse box is

Very useful if you happen to be out when the trip switch goes.

Teaching them how to sew on name tapes

Give them their own sewing box and explain that the eye of a needle isn't as impossible as it looks. If this is a success, start giving them their own little mending pile. If you're like me and can't sew for toffee yourself, a child who *can*, is a little blessing. Many people iron on name tapes nowadays. If your child is safe with an iron, show them how to do it.

Teach them how to read a railway timetable

Keep a spare one in the house so next time you need to know when the train goes, they can look it up for you. Saves a second or two if you're rushing to get out.

Show them how to look up names in the phone book and/or Yellow Pages

It's amazing how many adults don't realise that office names are in the front of the phone book first.

Go over some First Aid basics

For example, running a finger under water for several minutes if they burn it on the cooker. Even better, send them on a first aid course.

Show them how to clean garden furniture properly

Give them the right tools e.g. scrubbing brush, pail and garden hose. Make it fun by suggesting they do it in swimsuits and get their friends round to help.

Cooking

We've mentioned this briefly in the teenage section but even young children can learn how to cook providing they're supervised. Start off with making sandwiches and then toast. My daughter learned how to make a cake at the age of eight.

How to use the washing machine and tumble drier and other white goods

It's amazing how many teenagers go away to university, never having done this.

JOBS YOU MIGHT NOT HAVE THOUGHT OF

We've gone through quite a lot of possible jobs already but if your lot don't fancy them or you need some mental stimulation, here are some other suggestions.

- Plump up the cushions. A doddle but it might wet their appetite for something tougher.
- Sweep the front path.
- Pull out the weeds in between the cracks.
- Clean the kitchen floor. Make it fun by getting them to 'skate' on it with cloths below their feet to dry it. I do it myself when I'm feeling energetic or just plain sad. Even better when done to Radio 2.
- Change fuses in plugs. Obviously this is only for older children who aren't likely to electrocute themselves.
- Sharpen their own pencils at the beginning of term. And while they're at it, they could sharpen yours too.
- Shake crumbs out of the toaster. Again, make sure they're old enough not to electrocute themselves. You'll also need to show them where the broom and dustpan and brush are kept to clear up the mess.
- Get them to make a kitchen noticeboard so they can write down food you're about to run out of. If they've finished the marmalade, they write marmalade on it. Everyone in the family should do this and even tinies can participate. It all helps team-work.
- Water pot plants. Get them to carry them to the sink first otherwise you'll have water dribbling down the walls. Alternatively, provide them with a posh spray.

- Arrange flowers nicely. No, it's not wet. Tell your sons that future girlfriends will be very impressed.

- Sort out all those loose photographs that you haven't got round to putting in an album. Buy a couple of cheapies and get the kids to stick them in, instead. Make it fun for them by allowing them to write rude comments underneath e.g. 'Here's dad in the shorts he shouldn't have bought.' Ask/bribe/encourage them to file the other photographs in envelopes with the relevant date and location on it e.g. Brighton 2006.

- Make it *their* job to answer your mobile when you're driving. Not only will it teach them a few skills in telephone manners, it will also mean you won't be breaking the law. And it will set them a good example on how to be a law abiding driver.

- Get them to navigate when you're driving the car. Even middle sized kids can do this. Younger children could help print out a map from the computer before you go. Then they could follow the road while you're driving. It might also help their map reading skills. In fact, it won't be them who's saying 'Where are we?', it will be you…

- Ask them to wash hair brushes once a week. Show them how to let them soak in a washbasin of shampoo and then shake them dry.

- Make up a present/Christmas bag. You know all those rolls of leftover wrapping paper and stray greetings cards that you bought and never got round to sending? Now's your chance to get the children to gather them together and put them in a big carrier bag labelled 'Presents'.

- Make up a stationery bag. Providing they're not too young to swallow things they shouldn't, suggest they gather stray paper clips, elastic bands, writing paper, stamps etc. and put them all in a box or bag, marked stationery. Then get them to spell the word and make sure they know the difference between that and 'stationary'.

As my mother always used to say, the paper stationery variety has an 'e' in it, for 'envelope'. Well there's no reason why you can't teach them to spell at the same time as tidying up, is there?

- Sort out your small change. If, like me, you tend to have a pot full of pennies and other small change, it's a great opportunity for little hands making light work. Get some of those change bags from the bank and encourage them to sort them out. The prize is obvious. They get to keep the proceeds – providing there's not too much.
- Arrange books in alphabetical order. They might only get to 'D' before they're bored but it's a start.
- Write out your shopping list. They could decorate it too. And it will help practise their handwriting, however old they are.
- Clean windows. Ground floor ones only. For older children and dormant teenagers.
- Sort out clothes they won't wear or have grown out of.
- Encourage them to hang things up by buying plain wooden coat hangers and getting them to paint their names on them.

SPECIFIC JOB TECHNIQUES. IN OTHER WORDS, ARM TWISTERS TO MAKE THEM DO SOMETHING

Music practice

Routine is the key to this one. Get them to practise at the same time every day, just as they clean their teeth. It doesn't matter if they only do it for a few minutes. At least it's a start. Also encourage them by listening to other children playing. My niece was really encouraged in her flute playing by my eldest daughter.

On the other hand, is it really worth it? Gaynor Sbuttoni isn't sure. "Music is meant to be for them. If they really don't want to practise, maybe we should accept that they're not interested."

Getting games kit ready

This is a killer in our house. My trick is to have second hand spares of everything and keep them in the bottom drawer of my son's chest of drawers. At least, that's the theory. Again, it's so much easier if I get it ready for him but as I keep telling myself, that's not going to make him a very good husband. That reminds me. Giles – it's sport tomorrow so pack your bag.

Flushing the loo

This puts a difference complexion on the word 'job' if you'll pardon the crudity but it's definitely an important one. Again, try a Post-it sign on the door saying 'Have You Flushed the Loo?' This is one that's definitely worth calling them back for so it eventually becomes a habit.

Thank you notes

Give them nice paper to write on. If necessary, write them a 'master' thank you letter that they can adapt to suit whoever they're writing to (though ideally they should compose the master version). Make compromises. If they have written the letter, you might have to write the envelope. Well they can't do *everything* can they?

Packing their own suitcases

This is a tricky one because they are bound to leave out vital items. Still, if they don't start, they won't learn.

You could always pull a fast one by allowing them to pack and then secretly putting vital things they've left out (like swimming costumes) in your own bag to produce when they panic.

Top Tip

- "I keep a packing list for each child on the computer and print it off for them. I customise it as they get older. For example, when they stop needing nappies. And I remove irrelevant items like swimwear if it's a winter break. That way they can tick off as they go and can do most of it themselves." *Roni,* mother of three

- "When my children were younger, I got them to pack their underwear in a backpack which they carried and were responsible for. It meant that it was easy for them to find clean pants etc. in a hotel room even if everything else was all over the place." *Author*

Unpacking their school bag and packing it again

How many times have you missed a school trip/parents' evening/ charity fair because your child has failed to give you a crucial note at the bottom of their school bag?

Now you need never have that problem again. Make unpacking and packing the school bag part of their routine, just like cleaning teeth. Every time they've finished their homework, give them a short break and then get them to empty the bag and put in it what they need for the next day.

My 14 year old son used to do this as a habit every night before going to bed. But during the last term, we both got lazy and exhausted after moving house. So I allowed him to leave it until the next morning. Big mistake! It only added to the pre-school chaotic rush and invariably meant he left things out. Sometimes he wouldn't discover that he had failed to pack homework until he was at school and being told off for leaving it behind. This meant he would ring me in a panic and I would have to bring it in. After a couple of occasions like this, I got tough and made him pack his bag the night before.

Top Tip

They still won't do it? Put a little surprise at the bottom of the bag like a 10p piece or a small chocolate bar. Suggest that if they unpack their bag and pack it again, they might find something to their advantage...

IS YOUR CHILD UP TO IT?

Sometimes it's much easier to do something for our kids than nag them into doing it themselves. And sometimes, we just do things for them through habit when they're quite capable of taking on the responsibility.

If you've got into this rut, make a list of the main things you do every day. Then sit down with your offspring and go through the list, to see which jobs they could do – and have time for.

Treat it like a 'Job Specification'. The novelty might make them want to do these chores. The following list is taken from a brilliant handbook produced by The Family Caring Trust, which runs programmes for helping families. For more details, contact it at 44 Rathfriland Road, Newry, Co.Down BT34 1LD. Tel 028 3026 4174

Go through this list and tick off anything you do which you think your children might be capable of doing.

- Get them up in the mornings
- Make their beds; tidy their rooms
- Choose and lay out their clothes for the following day
- Dress them; tie their shoes
- Dress the baby
- Choose and buy their clothes
- Make school lunches; prepare breakfast; prepare their meals; cook
- Pick up their clothes; tidy away their toys
- Bath them; wash faces; brush teeth; wash their hair; comb hair
- Supervise their eating

- Iron their clothes; sew; knit
- Lay the table and clear it
- Sweep the kitchen floor; dust the house; vacuum the floor
- Clean and tidy the bathroom
- Clean windows
- Sort out and fold newly washed clothes
- Settle fights and squabbles
- Go to the post office/shop
- Do their homework with them
- Clean the car; change the oil; drive the car
- Paint the inside and outside of house
- Mow the lawn
- Dig the garden; plant flowers and vegetables
- Polish shoes
- Mend bicycle punctures
- Wire an electric plug; change a fuse
- Use saw/hammer; chop firewood
- Make the decisions about their routines, their friends, their lifestyle and their future

The authors Michael and Terri Quinn also suggests asking yourself the following questions:

- What are you doing for your children that they could do for themselves?

- What new responsibilities could you begin to introduce them to, during the next week?
- Be as specific as possible. Who? What? How will you start?

You might like to write down your plans.

The book also has an Encouragement Table to help parents make positive remarks instead of discouraging ones. For example: 'You've got five out of 10. Well done. I notice you're making a greater effort recently.'

This is better than 'You got five wrong out of 10. You'll have to improve on that.'

Other remarks to aim for include:

- 'That's it. Now you're getting the hang of it!'
- 'Now add in the egg and see what happens…'
- 'I see. So it's been very hard for you this week.'
- 'Oh well. We all make mistakes. What can you learn from it all?'

JOBS THAT AREN'T REALLY JOBS BECAUSE THEY SHOULD DO THEM ANYWAY

Wow. This is turning into a 'How to make your kid turn over a new leaf' book. The truth is that when I started, it seemed quite easy to define 'jobs'. But the more I thought about it, the more I realised that what I thought kids should do anyway, my own kids considered a chore. For example, getting up in the morning and cleaning their teeth without being asked etc.

So although these aren't strictly 'jobs', here's some hard earned advice on how to be successful.

Waking them up in the morning

Do this one in stages. Put an alarm clock by their bed. When it goes off, kiss them good morning. Set to snooze button. The next 'good morning' should be slightly louder and more demanding. Give them a drink. Encourage them to sit propped up in bed while daylight dawns. Have their clothes next to the bed. Give them a five minute warning. When they ignore this, tickle their feet. When this doesn't work, strip off the duvet. Then start screaming about how late you're going to be for school.

Getting them to clean their teeth

Of course they should do this anyway but it doesn't work that way. Make it a ritual that they breathe on you after breakfast so you can check. After you've cleaned your own teeth in the morning, put a line of paste on their brushes so you know when they've cleaned their teeth and when they haven't.

Talking nicely to older relatives/friends

The best way to teach them this is to start off by talking nicely to your kids. Ask them about their day. Ask them if they had a good one. If you find it difficult, pretend they're not your own kids at all but visiting children that you have to be nice to.

When your children learn pleasantries like this, it's easier for them to reciprocate. If they say they don't know what to talk about, tell them to ask questions of other people. Explain that older people in particular like talking about themselves. So they could ask them what they did yesterday or if they went to the library recently or how their backs are.

The great thing about this is that these elderly relatives will then be under the misapprehension that you've brought up your kids right.

Writing thank you letters

Give them some nice paper to write on. It might be an encouragement. Even better, slip some personalised notepaper into their Christmas stocking.

Get them to write out a master thank you letter with general information like what they did over Christmas. They can use this for each person with slight variations.

- Check the envelope. My children once sent the wrong thank you letters to the wrong people, each praising the virtue of the other person's present…
- If you're desperate, allow them to type a thank you letter on the computer. It's better than not doing one at all.
- If you're really, really desperate, let them e-mail or even telephone. I personally don't approve but at least it's an acknowledgment.
- As an alternative to a thank you letter, let them take or choose a family photograph taken at Christmas and write a thank you note on the back.
- For younger children, stick on shapes and make a collage card.

Going shopping with you

Yes, they hate it and yes, they drive you mad. So try:

- Giving them a copy of your shopping list and asking them to help you.
- Choosing a shopping time when they're not tired and hungry.
- Having a break with a cup of tea.
- Not taking too long. If necessary, go out another time as well.
- Promise them a small amount of cash that they can spend on themselves if they behave while they're shopping with you.

Washing their hair

If they hate washing their hair – and won't let you do it – see if they'll let an older brother or sister do it for them. Find out why they hate it. Are they worried about getting shampoo in their eyes? If so, you can buy non-sting shampoo. Try out those plastic halo masks. If they're still young, get them to wash a toy in the bath at the same time (as long as it's washable). Compromise. You squirt the shampoo on their hair and they rub it in.

Will you turn that music down?

Forget this one. You're better off doing it yourself. Or else turn your own music up really loudly. This could include the radio. Then tell them that's what it feels like. Alternatively, if you can't beat them, join them. Wait until their friends are round for maximum effect and then suggest they turn their music up even louder. Dance around the room and embarrass them. Hopefully the neighbours will then complain.

Shut the door behind you!

Just keep saying it. A bit like a broken record. Modify it every now and then with different levels of sound. When friends come round, keep going into their rooms and when you exit, leave the door open. When they ask (shout at) you to shut it, say brightly 'Sorry, I can't hear you.'

Turn off the lights when you're not using them

Just go round switching them off yourself (the Queen does this, apparently). Again, when friends visit, turn *on* the lights when they're least expecting it. Tell them you'll stop if they remember to turn them off.

JOBS WHICH, WITH HINDSIGHT, YOU SHOULDN'T HAVE ASKED THEM TO DO IN THE FIRST PLACE

Well, we can all get carried away, can't we? And sometimes we think our kids can do something which in fact they could, but can't be bothered to do properly. Here are some examples. For obvious reasons, the parents who told us about them didn't want to be named.

""I asked my 16 year old son to wash the dog. He did a great job. But he did it in the middle of our new sitting room carpet. I was sure I had told him to do it outside but my son was worried the dog would get cold. I was out at the time. Another mistake."

"My daughter offered to clean the silver. She didn't read the instructions properly and left the stuff on for too long. It looks worse now than it did before."

"I got my 13 year old to promise to vacuum. He thought he would empty the bag while he was doing it and cracked the case by banging it on the ground."

"I asked my 14 year old son to tidy my study and put all the papers on one side and the files on another. He wasn't listening properly and binned some really important stuff. Luckily I got there before the dustmen but it took me ages to sort it out."

"I thought my daughter was old enough to iron at 16. I showed her how to do it. I only left her for 10 minutes while I did something in another room and she managed to burn three shirts."

"I told my 17 year old son to use distilled water in the iron. I even showed him where the container was. Unfortunately it was next to a juice bottle. And guess which one he used?"

"I asked my son to clean the fridge. He did a great job but then he thought he'd defrost the freezer – while it was still on. He couldn't break the clumps of ice that were forming so he used a knife. He then cut himself and we spent four hours in casualty."

JOBS YOU SHOULD THINK TWICE ABOUT BEFORE LETTING THEM

DO THEM

- Light a fire without supervision
- Service the boiler
- Clean sharp knives
- Clean the oven with that caustic stuff that burns hands (unless they're wearing rubber gloves and you're standing nearby)

Feel free to add to this list, drawing on your own experience.

JOBS THEY CAN DO FOR YOU – BECAUSE (LET'S FACE IT) THEY'RE PROBABLY BETTER

There comes a time in every parent's life, when you suddenly realise your kids can do something better than you. This can be very depressing. But it can also be a great help – especially when it comes to jobs round the house. Here are some ideas to boost their ego and save you time.

- Buffing the bathroom taps. Kids have more oomph than many an adult. So twisting a cloth one way and then another is not as much hard work for them as it is for us.
- Setting the video timer. Their brains are wired better than ours when it comes to doing this.
- Transferring your Christmas list onto the computer and printing out labels. If necessary, get them to do this during the summer holidays so you're ready to go.
- Ask them nicely to wrap up Christmas and birthday presents.
- Cleaning windows. They've got more oomph. But don't let them fall out.
- Changing the ringer on your mobile phone. Showing you how all

the other bits and pieces work.

- Talking you through your new computer and showing you what else you could do with it, apart from the routine things you already know.
- Setting up an email account for you.
- Working the new camcorder/iPod/anything technical.
- Finding the end of that Sellotape roll (their fingers are niftier than yours).
- Picking you up from the station once they've passed their driving test.

Size really does matter

The Victorians had a point when they sent children up chimneys to sweep them out. Well they were exactly the right size, weren't they? We're not suggesting you do the same but there's no reason why they shouldn't use their small fingers and bodies to do things that we can't. For example, squeezing behind a chair to pick up something. Or putting a key on a key ring.

JOBS THAT SHOULD BE HABITS

How many times have you sat down on the loo for a bit of piece and quiet, only to discover that there's a cardboard roll on what should be the loo roll holder. And what's the betting that the previous occupant (who failed to replace the loo roll) is under 30?

This is when it's time to implement the 'Jobs that should be Habits' solution. It's a bit like the Pavlovian dog theory. If we can get our kids to understand that when A happens, B should follow afterwards, we might just get them to replace the loo roll.

It works like this. Pick five or six crucial habits that you'd like the children to get into. They could include replacing the loo roll/putting their plates in the dishwasher/taking off their muddy shoes when they get into the house/hanging up their clothes when they get undressed.

Now go back a step. What would they be doing just before you want them to do these things? If it's replacing the loo roll, it's using the last square. If it's putting the plates in the dishwasher, it's throwing down – sorry, putting down – their knives and forks. If it's taking off those muddy trainers, it's shutting the front door behind them. If it's hanging up their clothes, it's taking them off.

This is where the tricky bit starts. Every time they reach that penultimate stage, ask them what they're going to do next. Start off with a slightly jaunty tone. 'Aha, so you're home at last even though you're two hours late and dinner was ready ages ago. Shut the front door please. Now what are you going to do? That's right. Take off your muddy shoes.'

And so on. 'Aha, so you're finally going to bed' (try to resist adding 'after I've nagged you for the past five hours'.) 'Great, so you're getting undressed. Now what are you going to do? That's right. Hang up your clothes.'

If the jokey irony doesn't work, you might have to resort to a firmer tone or disciplinary actions such as taking away privileges. (Only half joking here.) The trick is to drum the pattern and habit into their subconscious, so as soon as they do the first bit, they automatically do the second.

Top Tips

- You can also substitute the loo roll for toothpaste. Not literally but every time they get to the end of the tube, they should find the new one.
- Make sure they know where spares are kept. Otherwise, they'll resort

to that old excuse that they didn't know where something was, so they couldn't do it.

And other habits to get them into

They've just had a bath? So they rinse it out. They've just been to the loo? So they pull the chain…

DESPERATE MEASURES

This is something I discovered by accident when my then 12 year old son and I were in a strop with each other. I can't quite recall the original reason for our disagreement but suffice it to say that it made us run late for school. I dashed out of the house to the car, laden with books and his sports kit only to find, to my fury, that he failed to hold the gate open for me. This made it very difficult for me to get through with all the paraphernalia which he should, after all, have been carrying. So I politely asked him to come back and hold the gate open for me.

He very impolitely disagreed.

So we had a bit of an argument which resulted in me having a teenage tantrum (even though I'm far too old for this), and declining to take him to school. At this point panic, not to mention reason, set in and my son came back to hold open the gate.

I'm not sure when we both the saw funny side of this but I can assure you that from that time on, he held the gate open for me. Now we are in a house that doesn't have a gate but he still hasn't been let off the hook. Instead, he will (on occasions) get out and hold open the driver's door for me.

I'm not suggesting you have a row with your children in order to get them to do things they hate. But you can make arguments work to your advantage.

FUN JOBS TO MAKE UP FOR THE ROTTEN ONES

Every good boy deserves favour as the piano prompt used to go. And it's true. Encourage them to get into job mode by giving them nice jobs to do.

- Allow them to give you or one of your friends a manicure. Yes, I agree it's dicey but little girls love this. Just make sure that there's plenty of nail polish remover on hand in case they spill it on the carpet.
- Permit them to tidy out your various bags and briefcases. Give them two carrier bags. One for stuff that's obviously rubbish. And a second for things which you will probably want to keep. Go through both afterwards. Their choices may not necessarily be yours.
- Sort out your makeup, tools, train sets, stationery drawer. As a reward, you can give them some cast-offs.
- Thinking of buying something new? Get older kids to price them for you on websites which show you where to buy the cheapest thing. Do the same with holiday offers and get them to find you the best value breaks. Make sure they print out and don't lose the vital information. Suggest they use this as part of their business studies coursework. You never know; you could be cultivating a mini Richard Branson.
- Get them to do a general house sort out and put unwanted rubbish in one room or corner. Once you've checked that no one wants them, allow your kids to sell them either on eBay or in a garage sale or car boot sale. Check the legality of ages and sellers first. You might need to go along. But we bet they won't be able to resist the opportunity of making money.
- Let them ice the Christmas cake even if they get themselves and the kitchen and the cake itself, into a horrible mess.

- Ask them to colour co-ordinate your wardrobe. Put all the blues together and then the browns etc. When they've finished, they could do their own.

Key points

- *Teach them practical jobs* that will come in handy
- *They might be better* at some jobs than you. Accept this gracefully and tell them how brilliant they are at setting the video
- *Write out job specifications*
- *Make jobs into habits*
- *Make a list of jobs you want them to do and they won't* Then use our strategies to get them to agree

Chapter ten

Looking after pets

This is such a big subject that it deserves a chapter of its own. After all, teaching your offspring to look after the resident pets is not only a useful way of sharing chores. It also helps them to learn responsibility. And that's pretty important when a life is at stake. So when the rabbit starts to stagnate, don't give in and clean it out for the kids. *Get them to help* even if it's going to take longer..

"Instead of nagging," says Gaynor Sbuttoni, "try saying something like 'I can hear the dog scratching at the door'. That reminds them that they promised to take him for a walk. We want children to start thinking for themselves and not just do something because we're nagging them."

One of Gaynor's friends has a picture of her daughter's rabbit on the kitchen cupboard door to remind her daughter that the food is inside. "You could also use Post-it stickers as well, saying 'Feed me. I'm starving.'"

FISH

Have fun cleaning out fish by taking them to the pet shop and getting stuff to colour the water. It might encourage them to do the dirtier bit like cleaning out the slime inside the tank. Encourage them to discuss cleaning methods with the pet shop staff.

When it comes to feeding fish, be warned by one of my own experiences which could have had a potentially fatal ending. My then three year old was looking round a nursery (with me in tow) when he decided (uninvited) to feed the class fish. He tipped too much in and the tank had to be instantly cleaned in order to make sure the fish didn't overdose and die. So if you are putting them in charge of feeding duty, make sure they know how much nosh to dish out. And if you've got one of those posh tanks with lighting etc, do check they don't switch the thing off at the mains in their enthusiasm. An entire tank of fish died this way at one of my children's schools. (And no, my kids weren't responsible.)

Teach them responsibility by giving them a fish apiece. They're more likely to take the feeding/cleaning rota seriously if they have a vested interest in something (sorry, someone) that belongs just to them.

CATS

Even smallish children can learn how to feed cats. Keep tins etc. within easy reach and also teach them the importance of washing out food bowls and washing their own hands afterwards.

DOGS

Again, children can and should learn to feed the dog. They can also be taught to groom but do make sure they do it the right way and don't end up annoying the hound. Wiping paws and rubbing canines down after muddy walks is another great way of dishing out chores that you'd rather not do yourself. It's probably a good idea to push the hand washing routine afterwards.

Taking the dog for a walk is something that all kids should do. But it's not always the doddle that it's made out to be. I have a friend whose teenage son was devastated when he accidentally dropped the lead and the dog ran into the road. Sadly the pet was killed. I only tell this salutary tale to enforce the fact that some jobs might not be suitable for some children. You also need to show them through several practice sessions what to do: how to hold the lead; what to do in traffic; how to cross the road safely with a pet and so on.

HAMSTERS, GERBILS, RABBITS AND OTHER SMALL ANIMALS

Clean out regularly; clean out regularly; clean out regularly. This should be written on their bedroom wall or at least on the side of the cage. Don't allow them to get away with it because it's quicker to do it yourself. One of the most important parts of keeping an animal is to learn how to look after it.

PONIES AND BIGGER ANIMALS

If you're going to take on a commitment like this, it goes without saying that the kids have to do their share. Unfortunately, even if it's their animal in theory, there are going to be jobs that they'll need your help with such as mucking out and picking out hooves. So think carefully before you give in to the 'I want a pony' argument even if someone offers to lend you a pony free of charge. When we first moved to the country, a canny farmer offered us his mare for a long term loan and my daughter couldn't believe her luck. Of course, what we soon realised was that looking after a pony was very hard work. And with the best will in the world, kids can't do everything especially when they start getting more homework. So think carefully before you add to everyone's workload including your own.

Key points

- *Only get a pet* for your child if you're prepared to spend time and effort to get them to help.
- *Use the responsibility* factor to get your child to help out. It will teach them the importance of looking after someone else.

Chapter eleven

Paid jobs outside the home

Even though this book is about things that kids don't want to do, we still thought we'd include this. First because there's a lot of confusion about what jobs children can legally do when they are still at school. And secondly, because teenagers often start jobs outside the home and then decide they don't want to carry on.

"Sometimes we need to explain that if we take on a commitment, we need to follow it through," says psychologist Gaynor Sbuttoni. "Obviously, if a child is really unhappy or the employer is not being fair, that's different. But an outside job can be a great way of getting them to swot for their exams. After all, they're going to need to pass them if they're not going to end up doing a boring job for the rest of their lives."

IS IT SAFE AND LEGAL?

When my son was 13, he wanted to do a summer job helping our local milkman deliver in neighbouring villages. I encouraged him, thinking it might instil a sense of responsibility. When he came back, he told me he'd had to cross several main roads and, on one occasion, tripped over a cat's eye and nearly got run over on a notorious blackspot.

I then discovered that according to the law, he should have been 16 before he'd been allowed to do the job.

Paid jobs outside the home can be great. But you need to make sure they are legal. Most children have to be 13-14 before they can do a job – and it's the employer's responsibility to check this. Just as confusing, each local authority has its own by-laws on how old children have to be to do certain jobs. And according to a recent report by the TUC, nine out of 10 local councils get the law wrong on teenage working because the by-laws need updating.

Many local authorities haven't updated old by-laws to adhere with changes at national level. For example, under the 1933 Act, children aged 14-16 can undertake light work, as can 13 year olds in certain circumstances. However, this should only be where the local council by-law specifically sets out the kind of jobs that they may do. Yet the TUC found that over a third of the councils responding (37 per cent) still allow children as young as 10 to work.

Many council by-laws also get the number of permitted hours wrong. Four in 10 (42 per cent) council by-laws contained inaccurate information on working during the holidays, and over two thirds (69 per cent) made a mistake on the hours that children could put in either before or after school. The Children and Young Persons Act says that 14 year olds can only do 12 hours paid employment a week during term time. Yet one London borough and 10 unitary authorities state that 17 hours is the allowed maximum.

According to the Children and Young Person's Act 1933, a 14 yr old (and where local authority by-laws permit it, a 13 year old) may not work for more than five hours on a Saturday nor more than two hours on any other day during term time. Nor may they work for more than 12 hours in total during the week.

During holidays, 14 yr olds (or, where they are allowed, 13 year olds) may not work for more than 25 hours during the week, nor for more than five hours a day. They may not work more than four hours a day without a rest break of one hour. They must also have two consecutive weeks during their holiday without employment.

If they are 15 or 16 (but have not reached the school leaving age) they may work for up to 8 hours on a Saturday during term time, but they can still only work for two hours on any other term time day, and still only a total of 12 hours during a term time week.

During holidays, they may work for up to 8 hours a day and up to a total of 35 hours a week.

If they're under 16, children aren't allowed to work as street traders, according to Section 20 of the Children and Young Persons Act 1933. But if children are at least 14, the local council may have special rules that let kids work for their parents in these jobs. Schoolchildren are not allowed to work in industry, according to the Employment of Women, Young Persons and Children Act 1920.

Complicated, eh? Confused? So are we. The TUC recommends that you ring up the local council to check on the law. You also need to make sure that your child's employer has registered them as an employee and has also covered them for insurance. An employer should also conform to the Health and Safety (Young Persons) Regulations 1997.

HOW MUCH SHOULD THEY GET?

Check they're being paid the right amount of money. Some unscrupulous employers will try to get away with underpaying teenagers. Ask around to see what the going rate is. The national minimum wage of £5.35 an hour only applies to 22 year olds upwards. Sixteen or 17 year olds who are not at school should earn a minimum wage of £3 an hour.

BABYSITTING

Amazingly, there is no law that says a child has to be a minimum age before they babysit for other children. In the absence of legislation, both the Royal Society for the Prevention of Accidents and the

NSPCC recommend that no one under 16 should be left to care for an infant. Parents can be prosecuted and fined if they leave their children in a situation which a court might say is 'neglectful'.

If your teenager does want to babysit, go over 'what if' scenarios and also get them to do a first aid course. It will add to their employability too as parents will be keener on teens who know what to do if a child chokes.

The Royal Society for the Prevention of Accidents has the following useful guidelines. It might be useful to show them to your children and discuss them. They are obviously aimed at potential teenage babysitters but provide some useful food for thought for us parents. Discussing these points will also make your teenager realise that babysitting is a responsible job – and not just an excuse for entertaining the boyfriend or watching TV. It's also crucial that children aren't given responsibility for another child's welfare such as looking after a child in the bath.

Good Practice for Babysitters

Note – these guidelines are addressed to children, which might make it easier for you to show it to them.

Sitting for younger siblings

- Do try and be open with your parent/s about how you feel about babysitting your younger brothers and sisters. If you have any worries or concerns, try to bring them out in the open. Try to talk about it calmly.

- Negotiate. No one can be expected to babysit every night. Agree to sit a few evenings if you, in turn, can have some nights off to do your own thing.

- If you do have to stay in with younger siblings for a whole week, ask if you can have a friend to come and sit with you so that you can share the responsibility of looking after the children.

- Try not to resent or blame your younger brothers and sisters for the situation, it is not their fault. Try to look at the situation from all points of view including that of your parent/s.
- Treat your responsibilities as seriously as you would were you sitting for someone else's children.
- Set up a back-up system. Is there another relative or other adult you can ask for help in an emergency? Would a neighbour help?
- Make sure you know where your parent/s will be and roughly what time they will be back. Give them a little leeway as it can be difficult to return 'on the dot'. Get a contact telephone number, if you can.
- In the unlikely event that something major occurs – illness or accident – would you know what to do? Do you know how to get hold of the family doctor and the Emergency Services? If not, ask a parent to help you find out.
- A knowledge of home safety would be helpful to you. Get to know the hazards and risks in and around your home. Identify the hazards which have potential to cause harm to you and the other children. What are the risks? Do you know how to manage and control those risks?
- If nobody thanks you or praises you for looking after your younger siblings, then give yourself a pat on the back for doing a good job.

Sitting for other people

- Are you aged 16 years or over and able to accept the responsibilities of looking after one or more children?
- Parents are seeking good child care in their absence. You must remember at all times that there is a child in the house in your care. Can you offer such a service?

- Why do you want to babysit? Is it for the love of children or to earn some extra money? Hopefully, it is a combination of both. If it is simply to get away from your own house so that you can do what you like in someone else's, think again.

- Take some basic training in the safe care of young children. Remember that young children are not only prone to illness but also to having mishaps and accidents. It is essential that you can cope with such emergencies. If you can study child development and first aid at school, do so; otherwise, take a first aid course offered by the St John Ambulance or Red Cross.

- A good working knowledge and understanding of safety in the home environment is important so that you can recognise good and bad safety practices. You should be able to identify hazards and risks.

- You ideally need some experience of dealing with and looking after small children and should spend some time with a family where there are small children present. Getting to know the child you will be caring for before you babysit is a good idea.

- Organise a suitable back-up system – such as having a near relative or neighbour available whom you can call upon in an emergency or simply to ask advice about an uncertain situation.

- If you agree to babysit, always be prompt and arrive in good time.

- Try not to let the child's parents leave the home before learning where to contact them. Ask for other numbers, too – e.g. family doctor, other relatives etc. You must feel safe, secure and happy to be left alone with the child or children before the parents depart for the evening.

- Know, in advance, exactly how you will be getting home after the sitting session. You might also like to negotiate terms of payment and whether or not you are allowed to have a friend sit with you.

Make sure you know what you can and cannot do in someone else's home.

COULD AN OUTSIDE JOB INTERFERE WITH SCHOOL WORK?

A recent report claimed that working outside school can reduce a student's chances of getting good GCSE and A level grades.

On the other hand, it can also make them more streetwise – and it gives them something to put on their UCAS form to show they haven't slouched around all their life.

As with many parenting problems, the trick is to find the balance. You don't want your teenager to be so tired after stacking supermarket shelves that they can't write an essay. But a two hour job at the weekend can broaden their personality and also bring in a bit of spare cash.

Holiday jobs are a great way of doing both. Employment agencies often take on teenagers so get them to investigate. Stores like Marks & Spencer tend to recruit several months in advance. The Post Office also has jobs for teenagers and students at Christmas.

Top Tip

My then 18 year old son claimed he was too exhausted after A levels to look for a job. So in desperation, I wrote this advert and pinned it on the village noticeboard. Luckily, he saw the funny side.

Lazy, indolent, exhausted (or so he says), post-A level student, reluctantly seeks summer employment at the instigation of his parents. No previous experience. Will consider anything that starts after he gets up (midday at the earliest) and ends in time for 'Neighbours'. Only available for ten days at the end of August due to holiday commitments.

In fact, he got a babysitting job out of it.

Key points

- *Holiday jobs* can be a good way of encouraging your teenager to stick at something/develop initiative/learn that it's nice to earn money.
- *Check with your local council* that the job your child wants to do is legal.
- *Be very careful* not to give your child too much responsibility. An older child may well not know what to do in an emergency. They shouldn't be left in charge of younger children if there isn't an adult on hand or near by. And there are certain situations they should never be allowed in such as supervising younger children in water.

Chapter twelve

Jobs we did as kids – without having to be nagged

"Setting the table and clearing it. Washing up. Boring jobs. There was no choice and no leeway. That's why I like to make jobs fun for my kids."

Sue

"We lived in a large Edwardian six bedroom house and at weekends, the three elder girls had to dust, hoover the sitting room and run an electric polisher over the quarry tiled floor. We often argued about whose turn it was to do which job as some were deemed to be easier than others. I remember once complaining that the sister below me never helped with washing up. My mum said she didn't push it because she couldn't stand her miserable face when she was forced to do it. At weekends, dad and I used to sing while washing up; we usually sang extracts from Trial by Jury because I'd done it at school and he'd done it in the army. One year in my mid-teens, when my mother had had another baby and her home help was ill, I did her job for two mornings a week for the whole summer holiday and was paid what the home help would have received. Apart from that, there were no incentives or bribery. We did them because we were told to."

Jan

"My mother told me to concentrate on homework and that there would be plenty of time for chores later. She was right!"

Sue

"As a child in the fifties, I did all kinds of jobs including helping with the family baking and also the washing which was done in a tube with dolly legs and a manual wringer."

Margaret

"I wasn't paid for doing jobs. It was seen (and this is the view I have as a parent) that doing the chores is a shared responsibility that the family just has to do. There is a responsibility to other members of the family to help each other and not burden any particular person with the responsibility of chores."

Brian

"I used to love drying up while my mother washed up because it gave me time alone with her. We had lovely long chats although I distinctly remember feeling uncomfortable when, at the age of eight, she used the washing up and drying up quality time, to explain the facts of life. Now, as an adult, every time I dry up a wine glass, I am reminded of her going into quite graphic detail about the ins and outs of sex (all puns intended). She was a nurse and believed in being open about most things. I've tried using washing/drying up time to engage my children in meaningful conversation but they usually say 'Oh stop it mum; we knew that kind of things years ago."

Jane

"When I was a child, I was expected to do everything including mowing the lawn and cleaning the car. We certainly didn't get paid. And we wouldn't have thought of asking."

Sara

"I was the eldest of five so I used to help my parents by taking my younger sister out for walks in her pushchair and playing cricket with my brothers. I always went shopping on Saturday for my mother so she didn't have to carry heavy bags. But I remember being told to cut the lawn and giving up because my father only had shears and not a mower. I wasn't very good at washing up either."

Bill

"The key is to start young. It's no good saying 'Now you're 13, you can tidy your room.'"

Paul

"My family owned a pub and we had to help out. We weren't paid but we were allowed to keep loose change which we found on the floor."

Dawn

"I made my bed every day and ran the carpet sweeper over my floor every Saturday. I can't remember how old I was when I started to do it. It was just something I always seemed to do."

John

"I used to clean the car with my dad and two brothers every Sunday. At the end, we were allowed to hose each other down. Mum didn't like this because we'd come in soaking wet. We've continued the tradition with our three girls."

Susie

"I used to make cakes and knead dough with my grandmother because her hands were arthritic. I loved it because she'd tell me stories about her childhood. It taught me what I wanted to do in life."

Sandra (now a professional cook and keen storyteller to her own children)

"I used to chop wood with my dad. One day, I cut my hand and had to have it stitched at hospital when I was about nine. But I don't recall anyone saying I shouldn't have been doing a job like that so young."

Clive

"I'd clear out the firegrate every morning for my mother. We had a real fire right up to the beginning of the sixties. I can still remember how the ash got into everything if you weren't careful. But I wasn't allowed to light the fire until I was about 12 and, even then, my mother used to supervise."

Pat

Chapter thirteen

Homework

This may not be a job, but it's still something they have to do – and we bet they don't always want to do it. So if you're tearing your hair out over a child who's reluctant to open their school bags (and we know the feeling), here are some strategies.

ADVICE FROM THE HORSE'S MOUTH (I.E. A TEACHER)

"Try to get them to do their homework shortly after getting home," advises Amanda Haehner, teacher at a London secondary school and spokesperson for a teaching union. "If they don't, they'll start doing other things and then run out of time. At weekends, when there's more homework, point out that if they do the most difficult bit first, they can get it out of the way."

Amanda also advises the carrot approach. "Ask them what they want to do after their homework and explain that the sooner they do their work now, the sooner they can do what they really want. Also make a copy of their homework timetable and stick it on the fridge door so you know what they're meant to be doing. Combine this with looking in their homework diary. They should have written down what they were told to do."

Organisation is the key word with homework, especially at secondary school. "When your children start doing coursework, they might think they have lots of time to finish it. Parents and teachers need to explain that kids have to get into the habit of working steadily so they don't miss the deadlines. It can help if parents can write down deadline dates next to the timetable on the fridge."

Hopefully you won't have to wipe their bottoms, so to speak, after a few months because by then, they should have learned to organise themselves. But we might have to do a bit of adjusting ourselves, warns Amanda. "Many parents get upset because their kids listen to music or watch television while they do their homework. We need to realise that kids have their own different learning styles. They live in a much busier world than we did and they have learned to fit more in. If they're getting reasonable grades, we shouldn't worry."

And if they're not? "Parents and teachers need to talk to them. Explain to your child that if they don't do their homework, they're going to have to face the consequences. They might fail a unit or an important exam. If you're really worried, talk to the year head and see if you can work out a strategy together."

ARE THEY SITTING COMFORTABLY?

Finding the right place to do the dreaded homework is also vital. "If it's difficult to work because the rest of the family is so noisy, suggest your child goes to the library or even a friend's house," says Amanda.

Even better, switch off these distractions, advises Bob Carstairs, assistant general secretary of the Association of School and College Leaders. "Ideally, there should be an atmosphere of quiet contemplation." (Good thing he hasn't been inside our house.) "There should also be a culture that's conducive to learning such as plenty of books and encouraging parents. If your children are going to do their homework in the bedroom, make sure they don't flick onto MSN when they're pretending to look up something for school on the net. You can buy filters to make sure this doesn't happen. Have a no-mobile-phone policy while they're working. And keep out any distracting brothers and sisters. It's also a good idea to make the occasional foray into your child's bedroom to make sure they're really working."

Funny he should say that. I'm a great believer in quietly checking up myself. But recently, my nearly 15 year old son has told me in no uncertain terms to get out of his territory. And although I don't like to think of myself as a browbeaten mother, it's sometimes easier to do as he says in order to maintain the peace. Mind you, that doesn't stop me from going through his homework diary afterwards to check he's done what he says he has.

GET THEM INTO THE SWING

Bob Carstairs also recommends establishing a homework routine. "Give them a bun and a drink when they come in but then jolly them along so they start their homework. Don't expect them to do two and a half hours all in one batch. They'll be exhausted by the end and won't give it their full attention. Much better to have about three bashes with short breaks in between."

Also show an interest in subjects you can understand. "Trigonometry might not be your specialist area but something like geography is fairly understandable," says Bob. "So you could try to introduce this into conversation."

ALLOW ENOUGH TIME

With younger children, find out what they have to do that night and fit other commitments around it. Don't have too many after-school activities or your child will be too tired.

BREAK IT UP

If your child feels overwhelmed by work, show him or her how to break it up into manageable bits within the time allowed. Sometimes it helps to make out a timetable.

DOESN'T UNDERSTAND?

There are plenty of educational guides for different subjects. There are also various computer programmes which help, although these can encourage children to wander off into cyberspace. Talk to the teacher and see if extra help is needed. My son's school does a maths clinic once a week at lunchtime although I have yet to persuade him to attend.

LEARN TO LET GO

There comes a time in every controlling parent's life when he or she finally realises they have to let go. I found this difficult too. When my older children had tests I would always revise with them and they didn't seem to mind. However my youngest (now 14) deeply resents it and makes a point of not telling me he has a test until after the event. I was hurt at first but have now learned that children have their own learning method. I've pointed out that if he does badly, it means he obviously isn't revising properly or hasn't got the right notes.

Top Tips

- If they hate French, get them to learn 10 new words a week, says Masha Bell, author of *Understanding English Spelling*. "That's what my son did. It helped him understand it better and he was surprised at how much more he learned. A foreign language is all about vocabulary"

- Do the same with English words. Practise one new unusual word every day and promise your child a small reward if he incorporates it into a piece of written work. Also use the odd French word in an otherwise English sentence to reinforce vocab. For example: 'Please make your lit.'

DO NOT DISTURB

If your child is doing homework, don't interrupt.

MOTIVATE THEM

Talk to them about their future, says Jackie Arnold, life coach. Find out what they want to do and discuss what exams and grades they need to achieve that. It gives them a goal to work towards. If necessary, shock them into real thinking by asking if they want to serve burgers all their life. Sometimes this realisation doesn't happen until their grades drop and they have to do something to improve them. Tell them they can only go out if they finish their work.

Get them to write down their goals on notices, advises Heather Summers, language and communication expert. "Then pin these goals on their bedroom wall e.g. 'My goal is to be a doctor. My GCSEs will help me get there."

CONSIDER EXTRA TUITION

Ask school if it can help. Or ask friends for word of mouth recommendations.

IS THE COMPUTER GETTING IN THE WAY OF HOMEWORK?

"Promise them 10 minutes on MSN for every 50 minutes of homework," suggests Heather.

NEIGHBOURHOOD WATCH

At the same time, make sure they are not hopping onto My Space or MSN when they are meant to be using the computer for work. This is tricky. Sometimes spot checks are the only things that work although they're not popular with teenagers.

BE AVAILABLE...

If your help is needed, says Masha.

BUT NOT IN HIS OR HER FACE

Try not to interfere if they don't want you to. Sometimes they have to learn by their own mistakes.

LET THEM READ WHATEVER THEY WANT

Well, as long as it's not the kind of magazine you find on the top shelf. Seriously, a comic is better than nothing.

NAGGING

This can work, says Professor Cary Cooper. "But only up to a point. It might encourage them to open a book."

ALLOW THEM TO FAIL SOMETIMES

Professor Cooper says, "Failure is the greatest motivator for children. All but one of our children went to uni but one of them got involved with a boy during her A levels and she didn't do well. Then she did her HNDs instead and went on to take a degree. So if they're not working, say something like 'It seems to me that you're not doing enough work. Well, it's your problem so I'll leave it with you.'"

DRAW UP A HOME TIMETABLE

This is Margaret Morrissey's advice, spokesperson for the National Council of Parents Teachers Association. "For older children I would advocate a discussion which produced a timetable scheduling in homework time. Ensure this time is when you, the parent, will be at home to supervise this happening. Don't let your children go out until you have seen the completed work. Ask school if they can email pupils' homework schedules so you know what is needed when."

Top Tip

Keep spares of pens, glue, calculator, mathematical instruments and so on. Very handy when your child has left an essential item at school.

IT WORKED FOR US! PARENTS' TIPS

"My nine year old son is doing a project on the Second World War at the moment and is learning about evacuees. They were only allowed to take a certain number of things with them so I got my son to show me the things he would take if he was an evacuee. It made the subject come to life."

Laura

"My five year old has one lot of homework once a week but it's quite a lot. So I get her to start early in the week and then break it down into manageable sections. That way, it doesn't seem so scary."

Caroline

"Set time aside when they must do their homework. Help them if necessary and offer something they want as an inducement."

Tim

"It's their fault if they won't do their homework. They need to learn."

Simon

"I try to help by supporting and encouraging my daughter. I make sure she understands what is expected of her. And I get her to recall how the task was achieved in class."

Laura

"I just insist on it. Homework is non-negotiable."

Anon

"If they won't do their homework I cajole, persuade, warn of consequences at school and then give up."

Anon

"I threaten to write to the teacher if he won't do his homework."

Anon

"We get them to do their homework with a lot of encouragement. Threats are counterproductive."

Jane

"I explain how long it will take and then what can be done, once it's completed e.g. going out to play."

Anon

"If your child has been playing on the computer or Playstation and can't seem to concentrate on homework afterwards, let them have half an hour off away from the screen to clear their brain before they get their books out. It seems to work."

Anon

"We have a computer spreadsheet for end of term results to encourage them to do their homework. There's one overall summary to capture the trend over terms and years with additional payments for term on term improvement. The other sheets are for each term."

Suzanne

"If they won't or can't do it, we help them."

Katy

"If there's a lot at the weekend, I usually get him to do it before seeing his friends. Sometimes I allow him to go out for a bit first but we agree a time that he must be home for it. Yes, he does stick to this!"

Anon

"My six year old found reading hard and frustrating to begin with. Forcing the issue only made it worse so I let her try by herself when she wanted to and helped if she needed me. The more confident she became, the more she wanted to do it."

Anon

"Remind them they will have to explain to the teacher why they haven't done the work."

Victoria

"I dish out threats to my 15 and 13 year olds if they don't do their homework."

Beth

"We set tasks to make homework more interesting. Last year, when my son's grades went down in German, we agreed he could have two terms to move the grades back up. If the grade didn't improve, we would pay for him to have extra lessons. However, when he got a new teacher, his grades improved. So it might be worth seeing if it's the teacher that's making him or her worried about homework."

Anon

"My two are at uni now and managing to fend for themselves, despite having done virtually nil when they were at home. This was my fault and not theirs, an attitude inherited from my mum who thought I should be free to get on with homework. The good news is they both seem to have turned into reasonable individuals who will shop, cook, give lifts etc. and help the place run a bit more smoothly when they're home. However, both their bedrooms remain no-go areas..."

Sue

"I 'help' our nine year old by sitting with him while he does it, rather than doing it for him. I also don't allow alternative activities like television and computer games until it is done."

Alex

"Set a timer. They have the set time allocated by the school. I write a note in the homework diary to say how long they spent on it."

Miranda

"I encourage our children to do homework by talking about what is exciting about the subject they're working on. I ask them questions and see why it interests them. I have always done 'older' activities with them like taking them to galleries and the ballet as tinies. Children can be stretched much more than some people realise and their intelligence is sometimes not respected. This is why they get bored. Homework has to have some purpose and excitement. For example, our five year old daughter loves ballet so we get her reading and writing about ballet."

Sophie

"We arrange time ahead when they will do their homework e.g. after tea, on Tuesday evening. We get homework out and all the equipment needed. And we tidy the table and point out it is ready for them so it's time to start."

Nick

Key points

- *Routine* Get your children into a homework routine. You'll know what suits them e.g. tea, a bit of television and then work. When you find a pattern that works for them, stick to it.
- *Make their environment comfortable* Make sure there's enough light and that no one's going to disturb them.
- *Be there* to guide them if they need you to. But not too much.
- *Motivate them* Talk about what they can achieve if they keep going.
- *Show them how to organise themselves* Wall charts; keeping up to date with homework diaries etc.

Chapter fourteen

What makes us do homework – and what stops us?

Who better to ask than kids themselves?

"I do my prep at school which is good in one way because we have to do it. But we often talk to friends if we can do it without being caught. If you get too much homework, it puts you off. Teachers need to remember that we've been working all day anyway."

Sam, 15

"We have to learn different words once a week. I find it difficult and I don't like it when mum gets upset because I can't remember."

Ellie, six

"My dad helped me with my maths homework but got it all wrong."

Sam, nine

"My room used to be such a mess that I was always losing my homework. Then my mum went mad. She put up a special shelf on my wall to keep my school books and said she didn't care what the rest of my room was like as long as my school books were there and not hidden under clothes. She only did this three weeks ago but it seems to have worked."

Alison, 13

"I do do my homework but my mum doesn't believe me. Then we row about it. She ought to trust me more."

Giles, 14

"I used to hate doing tables but then dad got me a tape with someone singing them. Now we sing them on the way to school and it's much better."

Oliver, eight

"The only thing that gets me to do my homework is when my mum nags me."

Will, 14

"I try to do my homework in my bedroom but my little sister keeps coming in and interrupting me. I've told mum but my sister keeps coming back."

Kieran, nine

"I find it easier to do my homework on the computer because I can look things up on the internet. Sometimes I go on MSN at the same time but it doesn't interfere with my homework. Mum comes in to check on me and then I have to pretend I'm not talking to my friends."

Sophie, 11

"We just get one lot of homework a week. Mum helps me sometimes. We do it as soon as I get it and then we do a bit more later in the week. I've only been late once and that was when I was ill."

Samantha, seven

"I'm tired after school and I just want to chill out. Then it's supper and then there doesn't seem enough time to do it all. Dad's always nagging me to start earlier but I find it difficult."

Kelly, 13

"I made my own personal organiser on the computer and wrote down when my coursework was due in and when my ordinary homework was due in. I stuck it on my wall and it's really helped to see it."

Ann, 15

"Mum never made me do homework. I always just did it. (I am a geek.)"

James, 19

"My parents didn't make me. I did it if and when I had to."

Andrew, 19

"I can only do my homework when I play my music. I'm always arguing with mum over this because she says I can't concentrate. But I do."

Max, 12

"I wish teachers would tell each other how much homework they've each given us. I'm sure they don't realise and then we end up with loads."

Margaret, 14

HOW MUCH HOMEWORK SHOULD YOUR KIDS BE DOING?

This is what the Department for Education and Skills recommends:

Years 1 and 2:	1 hour a week (reading, spelling, other literacy work and number work)
Years 3 and 4:	1.5 hours a week
Years 5 and 6:	30 minutes a day
Years 7 and 8:	45-90 minutes a day
Year 9:	1-2 hours a day
Years 10 and 11:	1.5 – 2.5 hours a day

Chapter fifteen

Pocket money – how to use it to get them to co-operate

Should you pay your kids to do things round the house? There are two ways of looking at this. If we do, they might expect us to pay them for lifting a hand every time we ask them to lay the table/clear the plate. But payment can also act as an incentive and a structure for a weekly family job timetable.

'Earning' money can also make children feel good about themselves, increase self-esteem and learn how to budget. So maybe the answer is to pay them according to the job. Draw up a wage table, writing down the job and how much you'll pay next to it. Some jobs can have the word 'Nothing' next to them because they're the kind of things they should be doing anyway.

One of the parents in our survey sticks a wage chart up on her fridge so her kids know exactly what they can get. 'I pay extra money for tough jobs like cleaning the car and mowing the lawn.'

BUT HOW MUCH POCKET MONEY SHOULD YOU GIVE THEM?

Dr Pat Spungin from **www.raisingkids.co.uk** has some useful advice.

"It all depends on what your kids want to spend their pocket money on. Obviously, your older child will have different needs to your little one but take the time to discuss with them the things that they 'need' rather than 'want' – and the differences between the two. Aside from traditional pocket money gobblers like sweets and

Pokemon cards, are your children (especially your eldest) expected to use the money for Christmas and birthday presents? Do you expect them to save? Has your eldest got a mobile phone, and if so, who pays for that? All of these considerations affect the final sum. Ask around – how much pocket money do friends' children get? How much are your children's classmates given?

"Once you've decided how much, discuss saving and budgeting. Again, this is more relevant for your eldest but even your five year old will be able to grasp the idea of putting away 50p a week towards a new toy. If you haven't already done so, open bank accounts for them."

WHAT'S THE GOING RATE?

Alternatively, you can get your mind boggled with national surveys on pocket money.

According to new research from Halifax, which claims it's the UK's largest savings provider, the average amount of pocket money is £7.82 a week. This amounts to a collective yearly spending power of £70m which goes a long way towards buying a few sweet shops.

Halifax survey covers children aged between seven and 16. The average weekly pocket money according to respondents is:

Seven to 11 year olds	£6.31
12-16 year olds	£9.15

Whatever you do, however, don't move to Scotland or you could find yourself forking out even more. The Halifax survey found out that Scottish children receive the highest amount per week – a staggering £9.23. At the time of writing, there was a big hoo-ha about Scottish children spending pocket money in the local tanning salon so maybe that's where all the money goes.

If you've got boys, you're more likely to be out of pocket. That's because boys in the UK receive 50p more pocket money a week than girls, on average.

If you're a total skinflint and don't believe in giving pocket money, you're in the minority. The survey shows that over two thirds (67 per cent) of seven to 16 year olds get some kind of filthy lucre from their parents.

Key findings of the Halifax research are:

Pocket money in the UK increased at 23 times the rate of inflation between 2003 and 2004. The average UK weekly pocket money is £7.82, an increase from the £5.79 cited the previous year.

- Pocket money has risen by more than double the rate of inflation since the late eighties.
- Most parents seem to give pocket money every week as opposed to every month until children get to 12. About 24 per cent of 12-16 year olds get monthly handouts. Increases in pocket money usually take place on a child's birthday, according to the Halifax, which is another reason for not showing your child this particular chapter.
- The Halifax Pocket Money survey shows that 56 per cent of children get regular pocket money from their parents and 14 per cent get it from grandparents.
- Around 15 per cent of children have to earn their pocket money by doing jobs around the home – Yes! Out of these, 27 per cent clean, 25 per cent do the washing up and 21 per cent do the vacuuming. If they read this book, they'll get some more interesting ideas.

ANOTHER SURVEY

According to another survey by NOP for the Abbey National:

- Children are earning more than £1,000 a year for doing jobs around the house. However, girls receive less than boys for eight out of nine household chores.
- The average child aged under 16 earns £1,200 a year from helping out and 21 per cent of parents with two children say they give away nearly £2,500.
- The most lucrative job is helping to clean the house, for which children earn an average £2.77, followed by loading and unloading the dishwasher, at £2.52. Boys are paid an average of £5.10 for this task, nearly five times more than girls' £1.04.

LEARNING TO BUDGET

If your kids are going to earn money through jobs, they might as well learn to save. Here are some tips on how to encourage them:

- Agree on a fixed amount to put aside every week.
- Shop around for an interesting savings package with building societies or banks. Many offer free gifts/clubs/incentives for young savers.
- Ask them what they really, really want – and then work out a programme on how to save up for it. For example, if they save up half the amount, you might be persuaded to fork out the rest provided they pull their weight round the house.
- When they get birthday or Christmas money, don't encourage them to blow it all at once. Suggest they put some aside for a rainy day.
- Buy young, vulnerable savers a gimmicky savings box to put their money in.
- Set up a swearing/bad behaviour money box in a communal room such as the kitchen. Divide ill gotten gains at the end of the month.

POCKET MONEY GUIDELINES

Fix a definite day for pocket money and stick to it. Use this as a tool if they misbehave. For example, if you don't do x, y and z, you won't get your pocket money on Saturday. It's more effective than threatening not to give them pocket money if they never know when they're going to get it.

Encourage them to keep a pocket money book, listing how much they've got and what they've spent. It will be good practice for the future when they're penniless students.

Give them somewhere to keep their money e.g. piggy bank or wallet (theirs and not yours).

Key points

- *Pocket money* can be a useful tool for getting them to do jobs they hate. But use it wisely. Don't hand out cash for everything. And don't be stingy.
- *Consider* drawing up a list of jobs and corresponding 'payments'.
- *Help them* learn to save.

Chapter sixteen

Facts and figures

To help with the research for this book, we sent out a survey to parents, asking them what kind of jobs their children did and how they encouraged them to do them. Just over 100 parents responded; the ages of the children these replies covered were:

Five and under	20%
Six to ten	30%
Ten to 16	30%
16 to 18	20%

Well, it looks as though some of our kids are a lazy lot. The parents who replied to our survey seemed to be divided sharply between the lucky ones who have children who help, and the unlucky ones whose kids would much rather crash out in front of the TV or send MSN messages to friends.

Below is a copy of the survey, together with the results. Many parents found that merely reading it spurred them on to get their kids to help more. It makes interesting reading ...

Do your children help with household chores?

41% of parents said their children helped regularly round the house

54% said it was 'occasional'

And 5% don't lift a finger

Which of the following jobs do your children do regularly?.

Tidying their bedrooms – 15%
Loading dishwasher – 11%
Cooking – 11%
Making own beds – 10%
Washing up/drying up – 6%
Looking after pet – 7%
Gardening – 6%
Helping with younger children – 6%
Vacuuming – 5%
Dusting – 4%
Cleaning car – 0%
Ironing – 0%
Watering houseplants – 0%

How old were your children when they started doing jobs regularly?

Our survey showed the average age to be seven.

It was nice to see that they started young – maybe parents were just desperate for help. Or perhaps it was a good way of keeping them amused.

Which jobs do your kids hate doing most? Our survey revealed the following:

Tidying toys/bedroom – 48%
Washing up – 8%
Washing – 5%
Cleaning – 5%
All of them – 5%
Cleaning the car – 5%
Ironing – 3%
Doing the laundry – 3%
Scraping plates for the dishwasher – 2%
Dusting – 2%

Do you try to persuade them to do these jobs by:

Nagging them – 46%
Paying them – 38%
Positive encouragement/incentive/game – 4%
Agreed to/expected of – 3%
Negotiating – 1%
Feeding them – 1%

If you pay them, do you:

Pay them different amounts depending on the job – 56%
Have a set pay structure – 41%
Forego payment – 3%

If your children don't want to help, do you:

Keep trying to persuade them – 64%
Give up – 36%

If the kids refused to co-operate, many parents also threatened to take something away. But one enterprising respondent played fast music instead. It's slightly unclear as to whether this was to encourage the children or calm parental nerves.

What jobs did you have to do as a child? Our survey showed:

Washing/drying up
Tidying bedroom/making the bed
Cooking
Cleaning
Laying and clearing the table
Vacuuming
Ironing
Cleaning the car
Shopping
Gardening

Were you paid for them or expected to do them for nothing?

Paid – 21%
Expected to do them for nothing – 79%

Do you think children 'get away' with doing fewer jobs nowadays?

Yes – 72%
No – 14%
Don't know – 14%

If so, is this because:

Parents don't have enough time to stick to their guns – 48%
Parents are too weak – 30%
Children are too stubborn – 22%

Are your children reluctant to do their homework?

Always – 9%
Often – 22%
Occasionally – 58%
Never – 11%

Do you encourage them by:

Helping them with it – 65%
Nagging them – 26%
Punishing them if they don't do it – 5%
Offering financial rewards – 5%

Do you help your children with their homework?

A lot – 29%
Occasionally – 65%
Never – 6%

How do you get them to do their homework if they don't want to?

Leave to them/teacher's discipline – 32%

Positive encouragement/reasoning/making it fun – 23%
Set aside time with no alternative activity – 20%
Nag – 8%
Put your foot down – 5%
Short bursts – 2%

These are the top ways that parents use to make their kids knuckle down to maths and so on. Also a couple of rather interesting respondents begged their kids to do it. We couldn't help wondering if they went down on their knees as well. In our day, we would have been caned for not doing it. How times have changed....

What other things do your children hate doing, apart from jobs round the house?

Shopping – 20%
Going to bed – 17%
Early wake up – 8%
Thank you letters – 8%
Walking – 5%
Adult parties/coffee mornings – 5%
Washing – 3%
Dressing smartly for outings – 3%
School – 3%
Music practice – 3%